1,000,000 Books
are available to read at

www.ForgottenBooks.com

Read online
Download PDF
Purchase in print

ISBN 978-1-333-40775-9
PIBN 10500708

This book is a reproduction of an important historical work. Forgotten Books uses state-of-the-art technology to digitally reconstruct the work, preserving the original format whilst repairing imperfections present in the aged copy. In rare cases, an imperfection in the original, such as a blemish or missing page, may be replicated in our edition. We do, however, repair the vast majority of imperfections successfully; any imperfections that remain are intentionally left to preserve the state of such historical works.

Forgotten Books is a registered trademark of FB &c Ltd.
Copyright © 2018 FB &c Ltd.
FB &c Ltd, Dalton House, 60 Windsor Avenue, London, SW19 2RR.
Company number 08720141. Registered in England and Wales.

For support please visit www.forgottenbooks.com

1 MONTH OF FREE READING

at
www.ForgottenBooks.com

By purchasing this book you are eligible for one month membership to ForgottenBooks.com, giving you unlimited access to our entire collection of over 1,000,000 titles via our web site and mobile apps.

To claim your free month visit:
www.forgottenbooks.com/free500708

* Offer is valid for 45 days from date of purchase. Terms and conditions apply.

English
Français
Deutsche
Italiano
Español
Português

www.forgottenbooks.com

Mythology Photography **Fiction** Fishing Christianity **Art** Cooking Essays Buddhism Freemasonry Medicine **Biology** Music **Ancient Egypt** Evolution Carpentry Physics Dance Geology **Mathematics** Fitness Shakespeare **Folklore** Yoga Marketing **Confidence** Immortality Biographies Poetry **Psychology** Witchcraft Electronics Chemistry History **Law** Accounting **Philosophy** Anthropology Alchemy Drama Quantum Mechanics Atheism Sexual Health **Ancient History** **Entrepreneurship** Languages Sport Paleontology Needlework Islam **Metaphysics** Investment Archaeology Parenting Statistics Criminology **Motivational**

..THE..

PRINCIPAL·DISEASES

..OF THE..

HORSE

CAUSES

SYMPTOMS

AND..

TREATMENT

PUBLISHED BY

H. S. BOSSART & CO.,
LATROBE, PA.

Copyright 1898 by H. S. Bossart.

NOTICE.

IN this short treatise on the Principal Diseases of the Horse, we have avoided all scientific and obscure words, and endeavored to make our language as plain and simple as possible, so that the most common understanding can get our full meaning. We wish you to follow our directions in every case: then you will be able to cure your animal without any outside advice or assistance. In return, we want you to speak well of Dr. Turnbull's Curine when a cure has been effected; give it your influence; recommend it to your friends: send the pamphlets to your brother horsemen, wherever you think they will do good.

The measure that you measure to others, the same will be measured back to you.

☞ We advise every breeder, trainer or owner of a horse to carry one of these books in his pocket, as it will be of use to him, and it will save us answering several thousand letters each year.

When this book wears out, or should your friend wish one, drop us a postal and we will send you another free of charge by return mail.

H. S. BOSSART & CO.,
Latrobe, Pa., U. S. A.
Sole Manufacturers of Curine.

FROM THE HOME OF THE GREAT ALLERTON (2:09¼), CHAMPION SIRE OF HIS AGE.

H. S. Bossart & Co., Latrobe, Pa.:

I have always been well pleased with the results obtained from using "Curine." It will certainly do what you claim for it. Yours truly,
C. W. WILLIAMS.

READ WHAT JOHN S. LACKEY SAYS.
Cambridge City, Ind.

H. S. Bossart & Co., Latrobe, Pa.:

Please send four bottles of Curine. I think it is the greatest goods I have ever used.
JOHN S. LACKEY.

DISEASES OF THE HORSE.

THEIR CAUSES, SYMPTOMS, TREATMENT AND CURE.

DISEASES OF THE TEETH.

DENTITION.—This covers the period during which the young horse is cutting his teeth, from birth to the age of five years. More difficulty is experienced in cutting the second or permanent teeth than with the first or milk teeth. The mouth of a young horse should be frequently examined, and if one or more of the milk teeth are remaining too long, causing the second teeth to grow in crooked, they should be removed at once by the forceps.

IRREGULARITIES OF TEETH.—In all instances where horses "quid" their food, slobber, or evince pain in mastication, they should be carefully examined. If, as is mostly the case, all these symptoms are referable to sharp corners or projections of the teeth, these must be removed by the rasp. We would recommend that the horse's teeth be examined once in every two years, at least, by a "veterinary dentist."

LAMPAS.

Lampas is a name given to a swelling of the mucous membrane covering the hard palate and projecting in a prominent ridge behind the upper incisors. There is no doubt that in very bad cases, and especially while teething, there is congestion and swelling in this part of the mouth which will interfere with feeding. Should this exist, the swollen parts should be scarred, being careful not to cut too deeply into the structures. Never burn the lampas, as it is cruel and should never be permitted.

DISEASES OF THE INTESTINES.

FLATULENT COLIC, WIND COLIC, ETC.

The most frequent causes of colic are, sudden changes of food, too long fasting and then feeding while the animal is exhausted; large quantities of green food, new hay or grain, food that has become sour, irregular teeth, and anything that causes indigestion may produce flatulent colic.

SYMPTOMS.—Horse seems dull, pains slightly, may or may not lie down. The pains are continuous. If not soon relieved, the above symptoms are aggravated, and you will notice difficult breathing, perspiration, trembling of the front legs, staggering from side to side, and finally plunging forward —dead.

TREATMENT.—The best domestic remedy that can be had is a dose of baking-soda, 3 to 4 ounces If this fails, give a half-ounce of carbonate of ammonia every half-hour. If suffering extreme pain give one ounce of chloral hydrate in one-half pint of water. A physic should be given as early as possible. The best is one ounce of Barbadoes aloes made up in a ball. Injections per rectum, of turpentine one ounce, linseed oil one-half pint may be given frequently to stimulate the motion of the bowels. Keep the horse warm by blankets wrung out of hot water every five or ten minutes and covered with a dry wool blanket. This will do much to afford relief. This form of colic is much more fatal than cramp colic and requires prompt treatment.

SPASMODIC OR CRAMP COLIC.

Spasmodic or Cramp Colic.—This is the name given to that form of colic produced by contraction, or spasm, of a portion of the small intestines. Causes—indigestible food; large drinks of cold water when the animal is warm; driving him when heated through deep streams; draughts of cold air, cold rains, etc.

SYMPTOMS.—It always begins suddenly. When feeding he is sure to stop suddenly, stamp and probably look backwards. He will soon get more acute pain and then he will paw, suddenly lie down, roll and get up again. There is then an interval of ease; he will resume feeding and appear to be entirely well, but in a little while the pain will return in a more severe form and may be continuous. He may try to urinate, but this is a way the horse expresses the presence of pain. It is very rare that a horse's kidneys or bladder are affected, nor should we, if a horse yields or sinks when pinched over the loins, declare that kidney disease exists.

TREATMENT.—Give one ounce of chloral hydrate in half-pint of water, or a very good remedy is two ounces each of sulphuric ether and laudanum in half-pint of linseed oil. If relief is not obtained from either of the above doses, they may be repeated. Keep the body warm with blankets dipped in hot water every five or ten minutes and covered with a dry woolen blanket, until perspiration is induced.

RINGBONE.

A ringbone is a growth of a bony tumor on the ankle. Causes—Injuries, such as sprains, blows, fast work on hard roads, jumping, etc. Horses most disposed to this disease are those with short upright pasterns, high calks in shoeing, too much shortening of the toe and corresponding high heels, causing too much concussion to the feet.

SYMPTOMS.—The first symptom is lameness, more or less acute. The ankle presents more or less heat and very often swelling. When in the front leg the heel is first placed on the ground and the ankle is kept as rigid as possible. In the hind leg the toe strikes the ground first, when the ringbone is high on the ankle, but the ankle is maintained in a rigid position. If the bony growth is under the front tendon of the hind leg, the heel is brought to the ground first. They are very bad and should be looked after at once.

TREATMENT.—Clip hair if thick. Remove all grease from part with strong ammonia water; immediately afterwards wash with vinegar; when dry paint with Dr. Turnbull's CURINE two or three times daily, for one week, then stop for a week, and if at the end of that time the trouble has not all disappeared, apply the CURINE again the same as before.

Wash with ammonia water and vinegar prior to applying CURINE the first time, but wash once every other day with warm water and soap prior to using CURINE, and continue to wash every other day, for one week, after you stop applying CURINE, to remove the scurf. Apply CURINE with an old tooth or nail brush. On very thin-skinned animals or horses that have never been blistered, you will find that CURINE used as above will take a very strong hold That will be all the better, and as the swelling goes down the trouble will disappear with it, but should the affected part show signs of breaking open, stop using the CURINE for a week and then apply again if necessary.

CURINE can be had from your druggist or harness dealer, or consult our special agents' list on pages 59 to 76.

BONE SPAVIN.

This affection is an exostosis of the hock joint. It may appear on the upper part of the hock or a little below the inner side of the lower extremity of the shank bone. This is what is known as a high spavin; or it may form on the outside of the hock and become an outside or external spavin; or the entire under surface may become the seat of the osseous deposit, and involve the internal face of all the bones of the hock, and this is called a bone spavin. With no enlargement to sight or touch an animal may be disabled by an occult spavin, which has resulted from a union of several bones of the hock. Spavins are hereditary, or may be caused by extra exertion, slipping upon an icy pavement, or an effort to recover his balance, sprains, and other causes.

SYMPTOMS.—The peculiar position assumed by the patient while at rest. The posture is due to the action of the adductor muscles, the lower part of the leg being carried inward and the heel of the shoe resting on the toe of the opposite foot. When driven he will travel stiffly, with a sort of a sidelong gait, and, on being taken to the stall, will rest with his toe pointing forward, the heel raised and the hock flexed. A little heat and considerable inflammation soon appears. The lameness which appears in backing out of the stall ceases to be noticeable after a short distance of travel. An examination of the hock will then begin to reveal the existence of the lesion, a bony enlargement at the junction of the hock and cannon bone, on the inside and a little in front and tangible to both sight and touch. As soon as you discover that your horse is getting a spavin, you should proceed at once to treatment and follow directions carefully.

TREATMENT.—Apply Dr. Turnbull's CURINE the same as directed for ringbone, on page 5. If taken in time you will get a permanent cure. If allowed to fully develop you can remove the lameness and sometimes the enlargement. When the horse is lame give him absolute rest while treating for spavin, ringbone, sprains, etc.

Beware of those 24 and 48-hour spavin cures.

BLOOD SPAVINS AND THOROUGHPINS.

The blood spavin is situated in the front and a little inward of the hock; the thoroughpin is formed at the back and on the top of the hock. They are round, smooth and well defined. In their general characteristics these tumors are similar to wind-

OWNER OF JAMES L., 2:11¼, AND LIGHTNING, 2:11.

Chicago, Ill., Oct. 11, 1895.

Gentlemen:—I have been using your Curine with great success, and consider it invaluable in a training stable. W. F. STEELE.

gall, although it is possible for a blood spavin to cause lameness and unsoundness in the patient if not treated as directed.

TREATMENT.—Blood spavins and thoroughpins should be treated with Dr. Turnbull's CURINE under the same directions as for ringbone on page 5. These troubles will yield somewhat easier than ringbone or bone spavin.

CURINE is the most powerful and best Absorbent, Antiseptic, Alterative and Penetrative in the world. No grease. Will not blemish or remove the hair.

LAMINITAS—FOUNDER.

CAUSES.—The causes of founder are wide and variable, the most common being overexertion, exhaustion, concussion, rapid change of temperature, etc. Founder from concussion is common in track horses trotting races when not in condition, long drives on dirt roads when the weather is hot, or when the change of temperature is great.

Overexertion—As rapid pulling or rapid work even where there is no chance for concussion. Rapid changes in temperature—Such as drinking large quantities of water while in an overheated condition, cold air being allowed to play upon the body when heated and wet with sweat.

SYMPTOMS.—Any one or all of the feet may become the subject of the disease, although it appears more often in both the front feet. When both forefeet are affected, the symptoms are well marked. The lameness is excessive and the animal almost immovable. When standing his head hangs low down, or he may rest his head upon the manger

WILL DO ALL THAT YOU CLAIM.

Allegheny City, Oct. 22, 1895.

Gentlemen:—I have used your Curine with the best of success, and I find that it will do all that you claim for it. W. L. THUBRON, Owner and driver of John L., 2:15, and Lady M., 2:21¼.

as a means of support and to relieve the feet; the forefeet are well extended so that the weight is thrown upon the heels, where he gets some relief. The hind feet are brought forward beneath the body to receive as much weight as possible, relieving the diseased ones.

TREATMENT.—The treatment of founder is probably more varied than any other disease. The body should be kept warm and warm drinks given, to draw the blood to these parts away from the feet; at the same time the feet should be placed in warm water, to increase the return flow of blood. In the course of half an hour the feet should be changed to very cold water and kept there until recovery is completed. Give three ounces of saltpeter in a pint of water every six hours, for a week, if necessary. If the animal is lying down, swabs should be used, and wet every half-hour with cold water. If the weather is warm, keep a little ice in the water. If at the end of five or six days prominent symptoms of recovery are not apparent, remove the swabs, and paint with CURINE around the coronet five or six times a day, and as soon as the CURINE has taken a good strong hold, which will be in a day or two, the wet swabs may be applied again.

FISTULÆ.—POLL EVIL.

The word fistula is properly applied to sinuous pipes leading from cavities to the surface of the

---

CURINE DOES THE WORK.

Chebanse, Ill., April 28, 1896.
H. S. Bossart & Co., Latrobe, Pa.:

Gentlemen:—Please send me by express another bottle of Curine, as I need it in my business. The bottle I procured from you has been a wonder worker in my stable, and hereafter I will not consider my outfit complete without it in my trunk. You are at liberty to publish this, as I think all horsemen should know of its merits. Wishing you renewed success, I am, Yours truly,

JACK CURRY (Driver Joe Patchen, 2:01¼).

body, through which a discharge is taking place. It may exist at any part, but it mostly appears on the withers. Poll-evil is a fistula and in no sense differs from fistulous withers except as to location. Fistula follows as a result of abscesses, wounds, bruises, irritation by the harness, saddle, bad fitting collars, etc. Fistula of the poll—poll evil—are caused chiefly by a chafing of the halter or heavy bridle; blows from a club or the butt-end of a whip, striking his head against the hayrack, ceiling, low doors, etc.

TREATMENT.—When the formation of pus is inevitable, this must be hurried as much as possible. Hot fomentations and poultices are to be constantly used, and as soon as fluctuation can be plainly felt the abscess wall is to-be opened at its lowest point, to allow the pus to escape as soon as formed; then inject 10 to 20 drops of CURINE, diluted with equal quantities of alcohol and water, twice a day, and, as the wound becomes more healthy, dilute CURINE in proportion.

FISTULÆ OF THE FOOT—QUITTOR.

Should be treated on the same principle as those already described. When fistulous tracts are found at unusual points, carefully examine to see if some foreign body, as a splinter of wood, etc., is not retained in the wound.

FROM THE PRESIDENT OF THE CANTON DRIVING PARK CO., AND OWNER OF PILOT BOY, 2:09¼.

Canton, Ohio, April 18, 1896.

H. S. Bossart & Co., Latrobe, Pa.

Gentlemen:—We have been using your Curine in several cases, and find it to have all the properties you recommend, and in my judgment is the best liniment and absorbent I have ever seen, and it reaches deep-seated troubles. I think it is a compound that should be in every stable.

Yours very truly, JOHN C. WELTY, Atty.

SPPUNG KNEES.

The flexion of the knee may be a congenital deformity and have continued from the foaling of the animal, or it may be the result of heavy labor at too early an age, or it may appear from too much substantial food and not sufficient exercise, and as a whole the tendons become contracted.

TREATMENT.—Paint with CURINE twice daily, over the tendons on the back of leg, from a little above the knee to pastern joint for one week, being careful to not get too much directly back of the knee, as that being a very tender spot it may become very sore.

If at the end of one week, after you have stopped using CURINE, no improvement is noticed, apply again same as before.

THUMPS—SPASM OF THE DIAPHRAGM.

"Thumps" is generally thought to be a palpitation of the heart. While palpitation of the heart is sometimes called "thumps," it must not be confounded with this subject. A spasm of the diaphragm, the principle muscle used in respiration, is generally caused by prolonged speeding on the track or road. The severe strain upon this muscle irritates the nerves controlling it, and the contractions become violent and produces the jerking character peculiar to this trouble. To distinguish thumps from palpitation of the heart, place your hand on the pulse at the angle of the jaw and watch the jerking movement of the body; you will see that the two have no relation to one another.

FROM THE BEST KNOWN HORSEMAN IN BALTIMORE.

Baltimore, Md., Nov. 8, 1895.

H. S. Bossart & Co., Latrobe, Pa.

Gentlemen:—I have given both your Curine and Hoofine a fair and impartial trial, and I consider them both the most wonderful remedies that I have ever used. MOSES MOSES.

Thumps is produced by the same causes that produce congestion of the lungs, and, if not relieved, death usually follows.

TREATMENT.—The best preventative for thumps is Speed Sustaining Elixir given prior to starting in a long race if your horse shows fatigue, and all race-drivers should have this remedy on hand. If nothing else is at hand, give half a pint of whiskey or brandy in the same amount of water every hour. Let him stand still and give him plenty of fresh air, have the harness removed at once, rub well over the body and legs; if the legs are cold, rub well with CURINE diluted with equal quantities of water. When the body and legs are warm, bandage the legs from the hoof up as far as possible. Throw a blanket over the body and let the rubbing be done under the blanket. Give an ounce of arnica in a half-pint of water every hour, or a half-ounce aqua ammonia (hartshorn) in a pint of water every hour. If no improvement is noticed in six or eight hours, the animal should be bled from the jugular vein. Do not take out more than four or five quarts, and do not repeat the bleeding. After an attack of thumps he should be well taken care of for a few days, as this may be followed with an attack of pneumonia.

SPRINGHAULT.

The symptoms of this disease is the spasmodic flexion, more or less violent, of the hock; sometimes almost striking his abdomen with the fetlock

---

THE OWNER OF PAT WATSON, 2:12¼.

Greensburg, Pa., 23, 1895.

H. S. Bossart & Co., Latrobe, Pa.

Gentlemen:—I have been using your Curine, and I find that it will do more than any preparation that I have ever used. Horsemen will never know what a good and useful article it is until they have once tried it. A. B. MOORE,
Owner of Meadowland Wilkes, 2:26¼, Pat Watson, 2:12¼, and Lady Crawford, 2:27½.

of the affected leg, and at other times lifting it only a few inches from the ground, but always with the same uncontrollable jerk. The habit is unaffected by the gait, and whether trotting, walking or merely turning around, it is all the same. The cause of this disease seems to be a puzzle to veterinarians and pathologists, and we will not attempt to give an opinion. We would advise absolute rest by turning him out to grass for a season and let nature right the causes.

NAVICULAR DISEASE.

Navicular Disease is an inflammation of the sesamoid sheath induced by repeated bruising or laceration. The thoroughbred horse is more commonly affected with the disease, yet no class or breeding is exempt. As a general rule one foot suffers from the disease, but if both are affected the trouble has become chronic.

CAUSES.—It must be remembered that the forelegs largely support the weight of the body and the faster he moves the greater is the shock which the forefeet must sustain. The result is that the coronet bone forces the navicular hard against the flexon tendon, which in time presses firmly against the navicular as the force of the contracting muscles lifts the tendon into place. The more rapid the pace and the greater the load, the greater the liability to injury must be. The faults of conformation most likely to be followed by the development of navicular disease, are, an insufficient plantar cushion, small frog, high heels, excessive knee action and contracted heels. The disease is also hereditary.

SYMPTOMS.—Before lameness is noticed the animal points the affected foot. While at work he apparently travels as well as ever, but when placed in the stable, one foot is placed out ahead of the other, resting on the toe. After a time he may take a few lame steps; later he may be lame for a part of a day and then seem all right again. In time he has a severe attack of lameness which may last a week, and finally he becomes constantly lame, and the more he is used the greater the lameness.

TREATMENT.—In the early stages the wall of the heel should be rasped away until the horn is quite thin, then apply CURINE three times daily for one week, same as for ringbone on page 5, or explicit directions, page 6. Then, if in summer time, the patient should be turned out to grass in a damp field or meadow, and in three weeks he should be brought in and treated with CURINE for one week same as before. This treatment should be repeated for two or three months. If in winter time, and you have no place to turn him out, let him remain in a box stall. A veterinary may perform neurotomy, but this may be attended with serious results.

HEAVES—BROKEN WIND.

Some eminent veterinarians maintain that the exciting cause of broken wind is due to a lesion of the pneumogastric nerve and there is good foundation for this opinion. The pneumogastric nerves send branches to the bronchial tubes, heart, lungs, stomach, etc., and all these organs may sooner or later become involved in connection with broken wind.

SYMPTOMS.—Every experienced horseman is able to detect "heaves." The peculiar movement

---

THE HOME OF HAPPY WANDERER, 2:20½.

Ethanmont Farm, J. H. Ellsworth, Prop.,

Washington, Pa., April 22, 1895.

H. S. Bossart & Co., Latrobe, Pa.

Gentlemen:—I have been using some of your preparations, and I find that they will do all that you claim for them. For Curbs, Sprains, Bony Growths, etc., your Curine has no equal. One or two applications will do more good than all the so-called spavin mixtures that I ever tried, and I think every horseman should have it in his stables.

J. H. ELLSWORTH.

of the flanks and abdomen point out the ailment at once. The cough that accompanies this disease is short and something like a grunt. If the horse is put to exertion the symptoms will be much plainer. "Smart" individuals become very expert in managing a horse affected with "heaves." They take advantage that the breathing is much easier when the stomach is empty, and also resort to medicines that have a depressing effect. When you are examining a horse and suspect he has been "fixed," give him all the water he will drink, and then have him ridden or driven up hill or over a rough road. This will bring out the symptoms of the "heaves."

TREATMENT.—Careful attention paid to diet is of greatest importance; always water before feeding. Feed nice clean oats, or a little bran can be added. Feed a small quantity of clean timothy hay once a day, and it is a good plan to slightly dampen all feed to allay the dust. Carrots or potatoes chopped fine and mixed with oats or corn is a good diet. Medical treatment is of a secondary consideration.

Arsenic is about the best remedy, and is best administered in the form of the solution of arsenic in hydrochloric acid (Liq. Acidi. Ars.), which can be obtained from the drug store. Give a tablespoonful mixed with oats and bran three times a day for two weeks, then twice a day for two weeks, then once a day for about four weeks.

KNUCKLING OR COCKED ANKLES.

Knuckling is a partial dislocation of the fetlock joint in which the relative position of the pastern bone to the cannon and coronet bones is changed.

CAUSES.—Horses with erect pasterns are more apt to knuckle as they grow old, especially in the hind legs. Fast work on hard race tracks or hard roads are causes for knuckling. Knuckling is produced by disease of the suspensory ligament, or of the flexor tendons whereby they are shortened. Young foals are very often subject to this condition, and it is largely due to the fact that before birth the legs were flexed.

TREATMENT.—Paint with CURINE twice daily for one week, over ankles above and below; allow it to remain for another week, and if not improved, apply again same as before. For young foals dilute three or four times with equal quantities of water and alcohol and apply same as above.

THICK WIND.

The great majority of horses called "thick wind" belong either in the class called "roarers," or are more affected with "heaves," and no separate classification is needed. Horses that are very fat and those that have not been exercised for so long that their muscular system has become unfit for work; horses with large bellies loaded with coarse and bulky food, emit a louder sound than natural in breathing and are called "thick wind."

The treatment is simple. Remove the cause and the effect will cease.

CAPPED ELBOW—SHOE BOILS.

Capped Elbow, commonly called shoe boil, is too well known to require any explanation from us. It is simply an enlargement at the point of the elbow, caused by the result of the pressure of the heels of the shoes upon that part. The peculiar position in which the animal affected lies down; excessive length in the shoe and the formation of the animal with a cannon bone so long that the flexure of the knee brings the heel in contact with the elbow.

FROM THE OWNER OF THE NORTHERN KING.

Waterville, Me., Nov. 22, 1895.
H. S. Bossart & Co., Latrobe, Pa.

Gentlemen:—Your Curine is the best article I ever used for the ills of horseflesh, such as Sores, Sprains, Curbs, etc. It is worth all the preparations I ever used before.   C. H. NELSON,
Owner of Nelson, 2:09.

Shoe boils vary in size from a small to a very large apple.

TREATMENT.—In small shoe boils paint over the surface twice daily with CURINE until cure is effected. In large shoe boils it will be necessary to make opening from below so that the fluid will run out; in this case inject 10 to 20 drops of CURINE diluted with four times the amount of equal quantities of water and alcohol. Inject once or twice daily until cure is effected.

CURINE can be had from your druggist or consult our list of special selling agents, pages 59 to 76.

LUNG FEVER—PNEUMONIA.

Pneumonia may attack both lungs, but as a general rule only one lung is affected, and in most cases it is the right lung. In many cases it is brought about by neglect and ignorance. A common cold or sore throat may run to pneumonia if neglected or improperly treated. An animal may be weakened from the effects of a cold, and when in this state he may be compelled to undergo exertions beyond his strength, or he may be kept in a badly ventilated stable, or the stable may be open and the body exposed to cold air.

SYMPTOMS.—Pneumonia when in its primary state is ushered in by a chill, probably overlooked by the attendant. His breathing becomes quickened and he hangs his head and has a dull appearance. The mouth becomes hot and a fever appears; if a thermometer be placed in the rectum the temperature will be found to have risen to 103° to 104°

ENDORSED BY A MEDICAL MAN.

Jennertown, Pa., April 15, 1895.

I have tried and examined Dr. Turnbull's preparations, manufactured by H. S. Bossart & Co., of Latrobe, Pa., and find them as meritorious as they claim. They certainly deserve great credit for placing such elegant preparations before the horse world.

W. L. WRIGHT, M. D., V. S.

F., or higher, (when in health the temperature of the horse should be about 100° F.) and the pulse may be beating eighty to one hundred or more times to the minute (the pulse of a horse in health beats about forty times to the minute), and the beating may be harsh or feeble. There is usually a dry cough from the beginning and a discharge from the nostrils. His legs are cold, bowels constipated and when dung is passed it is usually covered with a slimy mucus. When a horse is affected with pneumonia he does not lie down unless pneumonia is complicated with pleurisy, in which he will lie down for a few moments at a time. When a fatal termination is approaching all symptoms become intensified; he stares around as if imploring aid, the body becomes wet with sweat, he staggers, but recovers his balance. He may now lie down for the first time and may get up and stagger, and sway from side to side, backward and forward, and he falls to rise no more.

TREATMENT.—Place the animal in a stable comfortably warm, but do not prevent the access of pure air; make him comfortable with warm clothing; give him all the cold water he will drink from the start; blanket the body, rub the legs until warm and then bandage. If warmth cannot be established by rubbing, apply a liniment composed of four ounces olive oil, two ounces each of solution of ammonia and tincture cantharides.

Remove bandages one or more times each day; rub well and re-apply bandages; rub the affected side well with the liniment every three or four days. Give the following drench every six hours: Spirits of nitrous ether, one ounce; solution of acetate of ammonia, two ounces; bicarbonate of potassium, three drams; water, one pint. Never drench through the nostrils. Give a capsule of one dram of quinine every three or four hours when fever is at its highest. If animal is much debilitated, give six to eight ounces of whiskey in half-pint of water every four or five hours. Never give a purgative in case of lung fever; if constipation exists, overcome it by laxative diets, such as linseed mashes, scalded oats and bran, or grass, if in season. If the costiveness is not relieved by the laxative diets, give an injection of a quart of warm water three times a day. In addition to the laxative diet there may be given apples, carrots, or two or three gallons of sweet milk with a couple of eggs broken in it may be given each day if the horse desires it. Never force the animal to take nourishment; remove all food from trough or manger and try him with nice, clean laxative food later.

CAPPED HOCK.

A capped hock is the development of a bruise at the point of the hock, caused by rubbing or striking the partitions of their stall with their hocks, a habit which some horses have. The external appearance is sufficient to determine the diagnosis. They are an eye-sore and sometimes may cause lameness. If your horse is a habitual "kicker" and one that kicks when he receives his food, the best preventative for the above subject is to pad his stall, but notwithstanding all precautions, hocks will be capped in the future as in the past.

TREATMENT.—In the first stages of the disease, apply CURINE three or four times daily for two weeks, then allow it to remain for a week, and if by that time the thickening of the growth fails to diminish and there seems to be a fluid of a purulent character in it, open it very carefully from below, with a small instrument, and after the fluid has run out, inject ten to fifteen drops of CURINE diluted with four times the amount of water. In-

---

WOULD NOT BE WITHOUT IT.

Greensburg Fair Grounds, May 28, 1895.
H. S. Bossart & Co., Latrobe, Pa.

The bottle of Curine ordered from you some time ago has done the work. It discounts all other preparations that I ever saw, and I would not be without it if it cost $10 per bottle. A. E. RODGERS,

Driver of Patroon, 2:23½.

ject once daily and repeat as often as necessary, and at the same time paint over the surface daily with CURINE in its purity. You must have patience in treating capped hooks, as in these parts the skin is very thick and the absorption is rather slow.

CORNS.

A corn is an injury to the living horn of the foot and always appears in that part of the sole included in the angle between the bar and the outside wall of the hoof. Corns mostly appear in the front feet, because they support the greater part of the body and the heel is always placed first upon the ground, whereby it receives much more concussion than the heel of the hind foot, in which the toe first strikes the ground.

CAUSES.—Among the causes and conditions that produce corns may be placed the following: Flat feet which are easily bruised, high heels, bad shoeing, feet with thin horn, etc. Track horses going at full speed on hard track, and heavy breeds generally used for hauling heavy loads on hard streets, are most liable to this trouble.

TREATMENT.—The cause must be discovered if possible and removed. Pare out all the diseased horn, insert a plug of oakum in the cavity, saturated with CURINE, once every other day, and apply a roller bandage. Repeat until a new horn covers the wound.

THE MOST PROMINENT HORSEMAN IN AMERICA.

Cleveland, O., Jan. 7, 1896.
H. S. Bossart & Co., Latrobe, Pa.
Gentlemen:—Curine is the most efficacious remedy, and I gladly bear witness to its merits. I have used it and am using it now with the most satisfactory results. WM. B. FASIG,
Of the American Horse Exchange, New York and Cleveland.

INFLUENZA—EPIZOODY—TYPHOID FEVER.

Influenza is a contagious specific fever of the horse. It stupifies the brain and nerves. The disease is very apt to assume an epizoodic form, an attack of especial organs, as at one period the intestines, at another the lungs, heart, etc. It has been known in ancient and the dark ages of history to follow the track of the great armies all over Europe, causing great losses among the horses. It is more liable to attack young horses of from two to five years of age. Overfed, fat young horses and animals that do not have sufficient exercise are more susceptible to it.

The contagion will remain in an infected stable for some time, or it may be carried in the clothing of the attendant, or in being watered from the same trough or bucket. Creolol should be used as a disinfectant in all contagious diseases, such as influenza, epizoody, typhoid fever, etc.

Stalls, troughs, buckets, curry combs and all stable utensils used in working about such infected animals, should be washed in a solution of one part creolol to fifty parts water. The bedding should be sprinkled slightly with one part creolol to one hundred parts water.

A few drops in the drinking water three or four times a day will greatly assist in the care of the various fevers and diseases of the digestive tract.

SYMPTOMS.—The first is a fever, which becomes intense in a short time. Within a period of twenty-four hours the body may increase in temperature from 100° F. (normal) to 104° or 106° F. The animal becomes stupid, stands with his head down, and has no inclination to move or pay any attention to the surroundings. The pulse becomes high, eyes are puffy and swollen; tears run down and may blister the skin. If no other serious complications arise from the effects of this disease, a change for the better may be anticipated after about the seventh day.

TREATMENT.—Place the animal in a comfortable stall away from the other horses if possible.

Give small doses of Glauber or Epsom salts, to which may be added a little bicarbonate of soda, from the start, in order to prevent constipation and its evil results, but should diarrhœa become too great, you should overcome this by giving drinks made from boiled starch or rice, to which may be added one ounce of laudanum, every three or four hours. When fever is observed to be rising rapidly give two or three doses of quinine in ¼-dram capsules, or ½ dram of antimony every three or four hours. This will reduce the high fever. If depression is great after quinine or antimony is given, fluid extract of aconite may be given in doses of ten to twenty drops every three or four hours. In complication of the lungs give ten to twenty drops of fluid extract of digitalis every four hours. The best way to administer medicines in small doses is with a small syringe, placed in the side of the mouth and thrown on the tongue. If the appetite remains, give moderate quantities of good hay and laxative foods, such as oats, bran mashes, etc.

WINDPUFFS—WINDGALLS.

Windpuffs.—These eye-sores appear in the form of soft tumors at the posterior part of the fetlock joint and are generally of a round appearance. They sometimes cause lameness when they are large enough to interfere with the tendons, or when they undergo a change, such as calcification, which they

---

THE SECRETARY OF THE DRIVING PARK.

Johnstown, Pa., May 8, 1895.

H. S. Bossart & Co., Latrobe, Pa.

Gentlemen:—The Curine and Hoofine ordered from you some time ago, duly to hand, and the application of the same has proven all you claim for their separate curatives, and I cheerfully recommend them to owners and drivers of horses of all kinds. There are a number of trainers at our track, and Curine and Hoofine are to be found in all their stables, which fact talks for itself.

Yours very truly, W. S. STEELE,
Secretary of Johnstown Driving Park.

are likely to do. They may be attributed to external causes, such as strains from heavy pulling, fast driving, jumping. etc.

TREATMENT.—When in their acute stage, paint with CURINE twice daily for one week, and you will have accomplished all that will be desired. If the animal is in training, apply a cold water bandage for one hour after work, remove and when dry paint with CURINE diluted with equal quantities of water and alcohol, once daily. If the trouble has become chronic and the enlargement of long duration, apply CURINE twice daily for one week, then let it remain for another week, and if the trouble has not all disappeared apply CURINE again, same as before. Wash every other day with warm water and soap, prior to using the compound, and when dry apply the paint.

LOCK-JAW—TETANIS.

Lock-Jaw is characterized by spasms affecting the muscles of the body, legs, face and neck, of all the muscles supplied by the cerebrospinal nerves.

CAUSES.—It is mostly caused by wounds, especially pricks or wounds of the feet. It sometimes follows castration or docking, and may not appear for two or three months after the wound has healed. Horses of a nervous disposition are more subject to it than those of a sluggish nature, and stallions are more apt to develop tetanis, as a result of wounds, than geldings or mares.

SYMPTOMS.—The first symptom that you will notice is difficulty in chewing and swallowing, an elevation of the head, etc. An examination of the mouth will reveal his inability to open it to its full

---

CURINE IS INVALUABLE.

Graham, N. C., May 29, 1895.
H. S. Bossart & Co., Latrobe, Pa.
Gentlemen:—We think your Curine is invaluable.
L. B. HOLT & CO.,
Former owners of John R. Gentry, 2:00½.

extent. The muscles become rigid; tail usually elevated. These symptoms become aggravated and the muscles rigid. Jaws completely set; nostrils dilated, and he presents a picture of great agony until death relieves him. All symptoms may increase for eight to ten days, and then diminish under judicial treatment.

TREATMENT.—The animal should be placed in a box stall in as quiet a place as possible. Remove all bedding; keep the place moderately dark and the attendant must be as quiet as possible about him. Give him one ounce of Barbadoes aloes made up in form of a ball, or a quart of raw linseed oil. If the jaws are set and you cannot open his mouth sufficiently, dissolve the aloes in a couple ounces of sweet oil and throw on the back of the tongue with a syringe. If the jaws are set give an injection under the skin every four hours, of one-fourth of a grain of atropia and five grains of sulphate of morphia dissolved in one dram of water. Keep a pail of water constantly before him, placed high, so he can put his mouth in it without exerting himself. If he is unable to swallow inject gruel and milk into the rectum in order to keep his strength up.

CURB.

Curb.—This lesion is the bulging backward of the posterior part of the hock. It may be caused by a sprain of the strong ligament or tendon on the back part of the hock. This condition is mostly found on hocks of a curby nature. It may also be caused by slipping, jumping or pulling heavy loads.

FROM A PRACTICAL MAN.

Pittsburg, Pa., Oct. 25, 1895.
H. S. Bossart & Co.

Gentlemen:—I have been using your Curine, and I find it the best preparation that I have ever seen or used. CLARENCE HENDERSON,
Owner and driver of Frank T., 2:17¼, and Maud E., 2:19¼.

A curb is an "unsoundness,". as the hock thus affected is less liable to endure severe labor.

TREATMENT.—On the first appearance of a curb subdue the inflammation by the use of hot fomentations, then paint with Dr. Turnbull's CURINE over the affected part, twice a day for one week; wash every other day with warm water and soap, and when dry apply CURINE. In curbs of long standing it may be necessary to repeat the treatment for a couple of weeks.

SPLINTS.

A splint is a certain bony enlargement which is developed on the cannon bone between the knee or hock and the fetlock joint and are usually found on the inside of the leg. They vary in size from that of a large nut to merely nothing, and in searching for them they may be easily detected by the hand, but must be distinguished from a small enlargement at the lower third of the cannon bone, which is no splint, but merely a normal development of the small cannon bone. A splint may frequently cause lameness, and when near the knee-joint the lameness is more apt to become aggravated.

CAUSES.—Splints are mostly caused by external hurts, such as blows or collisions, or in speeding he may strike the inside of his leg with his opposite foot and thus start the growth; or too much excessive strain or labor upon a young animal at a too early period in his life.

THE BEST REMEDY.

Elyria Stock Farm, Elyria, O., Oct. 23, 1895.

Gentlemen:—I have been using your Curine, and am pleased to say it is the best remedy for Splints, Curbs, Ringbones, etc., that I have ever used, and I think no stable complete without it.

FRANK P. DOBLE,
Driver of Gertrude, 2:12; Peveril, 2:14, etc.

TREATMENT.—As soon as the splint is located, paint with CURINE twice daily for one week. If of long standing it will have become almost as hard as bone and you will probably have to keep the treatment up for two or three weeks.

SORES—SUMMER SORES.

These sores are small at first and may appear at any point, but they are more likely to appear on the legs or where the harness presses on the body. These sores contain parasites and cause intense itching, and the victim rubs and bites them until extensive raw surfaces are produced.

TREATMENT.—Place in a cool place and sponge very carefully with cold water; then, in order to remove the pus and kill the parasite, paint with CURINE and then cover the surface of the wound by dusting it with iodoform. Repeat once a day for two weeks or until the sore heals up, as these wounds are very obstinate and often require months to heal.

RUPTURE OF THE SUSPENSORY LIGAMENT.

Sprain, with or without rupture, of the suspensory ligament, may happen in any leg. Old animals and especially trotters, paces and runners, are the most subject to this injury, and the trouble is nearly always in one, or both, fore legs. Horses used for heavy draught are more liable to have the hind leg affected. One, or both, of the branches may be torn from their attachment to the sesamoid bones; or the ligament may rupture above the point of division.

TREATMENT.—No matter how mild the sprain of the suspensory ligament may be, it should always be treated with enforced rest for a month. Bathe thoroughly at once with cold water, and apply cold water bandages until the fever has subsided, then paint with CURINE twice a day for one week; now let it remain for one week, but during this time wash it every other day with warm water and soap. Paint with CURINE for another week, same as before, and the following week wash again with warm water and soap. At the end of one month from the time he was laid up, he may be able to walk around slowly. It will be useless to expect a removal of all the thickening, for new tissues have formed, and it will always remain somewhat enlarged.

BOTS.

Cobbold, who is considered the best authority on this subject, says: "The common gad-fly attacks the animal while grazing late in the summer, its object being, not to derive sustenance, but to deposit its eggs. This is accomplished by means of a glutinous excretion, causing the ova (eggs) to adhere to the hairs. The parts selected are chiefly those of the shoulder, base of the neck, and inner part of the fore legs, especially about the knees, for in these situations the horse will have no difficulty in reaching the ova with its tongue. When the animal licks those parts of the coat where the eggs have been placed the moisture of the tongue, aided by warmth, hatches the ova, and in something less than three weeks from the time of the deposition of the eggs the larvae have made their escape. As maggots they are next transferred to the mouth and ultimately to the stomach along with food and drink. A great many larvae perish during this passive mode of immigration, some being dropped from the mouth and others being crushed in the fodder during mastication. It has been calculated that out of the many hundreds of eggs deposited on a single horse scarcely one out of fifty of the larvae arrive within the stomach. Notwithstanding this waste the interior of the stomach may become completely covered (cuticular portion) with bots. Whether there be few or many they are anchored in this situation chiefly by means of two large cephalic hooks. After the bots have attained perfect growth they voluntarily loosen their hold and allow themselves to be carried along the alimentary canal until they escape with the feces. In all cases they sooner or later fall to the ground and when transferred to the soil they bury themselves beneath the surface in order to undergo transformation into the pupa condition. Having remained in the earth for a period of six or seven weeks they finally emerge from their pupal-cocoons as perfect dipterus (winged) insects, the gad-fly. It thus appears that bots ordinarily pass about eight months of their lifetime in the digestive organs of the horse."

It is a very common expression to hear bystanders exclaim: "Your horse has the bots," when the animal is suffering from some internal pain. Bots in large numbers may interfere somewhat with digestion, but beyond this they are as a general thing harmless. They loosen their hold during the spring months and pass out in large numbers, but so far as medicine is concerned, none is necessary. In order to prevent the horse from having bots, it would be necessary to scrape off all the eggs deposited by the gad-fly and destroy them.

OVERREACH.

This trouble is caused by the shoe of the hind foot striking the quarters or heel of the fore foot. It mostly happens when the animal is going at speed and is more common among trotters, pacers and runners.

SYMPTOMS.—The quarter or heel is cut and bruised, or the horse may grab and pull his front shoe off. Horses accustomed to overreaching are very "bad breakers," owing to the pain which excites them.

TREATMENT.—If the parts are cut, bathe thoroughly with cold water, and dress the wound with CURINE diluted with three to four times water, place a little cotton or oakum over the wound and apply a cold damp roller bandage. This should be repeated once daily for one week. If only a bruise, apply CURINE as above and use a cold wet bandage for a couple of days.

WORMS.

There are several species of worms found in the intestines, and they appear most frequently in young, weak and debilitated animals.

SYMPTOMS.—Depraved appetite, bowels irregular, hide bound, pot bellied, bat coat, hair standing up, etc. The best symptoms is seeing the animal pass them in his dung.

TREATMENT.—Feed bran mashes for a day or two and then give the following: Tartar emetic six drams, calomel one dram; mix and divide into six powders and give one each day in his feed. No physic necessary. If pin worms are present, inject into the rectum an infusion of tobacco once a day for a few days.

SHOULDER LAMENESS.

Shoulder lameness.—This trouble is most frequently caused by a sprain lacerating the muscles, tendons, or the ligaments of the joint. The sprain may be caused by slipping, starting a heavy load, jumping, a quick muscular movement, or from a powerful concussion.

WORTH ONE HUNDRED DOLLARS TO THEM.
        Hammond, Ind., Jan. 23, 1896.
H. S. BOSSART & CO., Latrobe, Pa.

Gentlemen.—In three weeks Curine removed an enlargement on a valuable colt's leg. Prior to this we had doctored him for one year without any effect whatever. The one bottle was worth one hundred dollars to us, and we think that every horseman in the land should know of its merits. Please send us six bottles, as we want to sell it for you.
        Yours truly,
            J. B. SMITH & CO.,
                Wholesale and Retail Grocers.

SYMPTOMS.—Continual lameness and sometimes swelling will appear at the point of injury. The peculiar swinging manner in which he carries his leg forward while trotting or walking. In backing him he will sometimes drag the whole leg, seemingly without any motion in the upper part.

TREATMENT.—If the lameness is severe, give the animal rest; bathe the shoulder thoroughly with warm water twice a day, and when dry, paint with DR. TURNBULL'S CURINE. Repeat twice a day for one week, then allow it to remain for one week and if the lameness is not entirely removed apply the same treatment for another week. If the lameness is not severe and the horse must be worked, apply CURINE once a day for one week.

CALK WOUNDS.

Animals wearing sharp calks are liable to strike or tramp themselves about the coronary regions. Driving horses calked for driving on icy roads are very apt to strike the quarters of the front feet, while in the hind feet, the wound often results from the animal resting with the heel of one foot on the front of the other.

TREATMENT.—Follow the same treatment as directed for overreach on page 28.

THRUSH.

Thrush is a disease caused by a secretion of unhealthy matter from the cleft of the frog. City

---

FROM A VERY PROMINENT HORSEMAN IN ONTARIO.

Richmond, Ont., Jan. 28th, 1896.

H. S. BOSSART & CO., Latrobe, Pa.

Gentlemen:—This is to certify that I have used your Curine and must say it is the greatest medicine I have ever used for lameness in horses of any kind, and particularly for thrush. It will cure any case of thrush in five days. I can't get along without it. Yours truly, J. H. LANE.

horses are more subject to this disease than country horses, owing to them remaining in filthy stables.

CAUSES.—Animals standing in filthy stalls; sudden changes of dryness to excessive moisture. Hard driving on rough roads may also induce this disease.

SYMPTOMS.—An offensive smell in the cleft of the frog; later a watery discharge, changing to a mattery substance, and as the case becomes older, lameness may be noticed.

TREATMENT.—Keep the stall clean. Cut the diseased portion of the horn away, clean the cleft of the frog thoroughly, then saturate the cleft and grooves well with CURINE and dress with roller bandage or leather boot to keep the dirt out. Repeat once daily for one week. Keep the boot or bandage on for another week and if a cure is not effected, repeat for another week.

SCRATCHES—CRACKED HEELS.

This usually starts with heat and swelling in the hollow of the heel, with stiffness and lameness in many cases; slight cracks with a tendency to enlarge soon appear. It may extend from the back of the knee, or hock, to the hoof.

CAUSES.—Imperfect nourishment, cold draughts, snow, and freezing mud, hot and dirty stables, overfeeding on grain, washing the legs and failing to thoroughly dry them, or wrapping the legs in

---

THE OWNER OF CORPORAL, 2:12½.

Columbus, Neb., April 28, 1897.

H. S. Bossart & Co., Latrobe, Pa.

Gentlemen:—During the spring meeting at Denver in 1896 my horse, the Corporal, went lame in a race. I tried everything last summer to cure him, but with no success. During this spring I bought a bottle of Curine, and in ten days he was working as sound as a dollar. Yours truly,

C. E. MORSE.

wool bandages before they are dry, clipping the heels, or long hair from pastern, etc.

TREATMENT.—Remove all dirt thoroughly with warm water, and when well dried paint with CURINE twice daily for one week, diluted with two to four times equal quantities water and alcohol. Bandage with a dry cotton bandage. Give a small handful of Epsom or Glauber salts in feed, twice a day for a week or so.

PULSE.

The Pulse or Heart in standard or thoroughbred horses, when in health and at complete rest, should beat forty to forty-five times in a minute, while in a heavy or coarse-bred animal it may only beat thirty-five to forty times a minute. Work or excitement increases the pulsation.

RESPIRATION.

A horse, when at complete rest and in good health, breathes thirteen to fifteen times in a minute. Excitement or work will increase the breathing.

TEMPERATURE.

The temperature of a horse in health may be placed at about 100° F. Standard and thoroughbreds may be as high as 101° F. Mares have a higher temperature than stallions or geldings. Exercise increases the temperature.

BIG LEG—LYMPHANGITIS.

Big Leg.—This disease is an inflammation of the lymphatic structures and mostly appears in the hind leg. It is very sudden and painful, accompanied with a high temperature.

SYMPTOMS.—Animal becomes chilly with rising temperature, followed by lameness and swelling. The swelling appears at the inside of the thigh and continues down to the foot. The swelling and temperature will increase for a couple of days and then commence to recede. It generally leaves a permanent enlargement, unless very careful attention is given the animal.

TREATMENT.—Bathe the leg well with strong ammonia water, to which add about one quart of vinegar to each gallon. Bathe thoroughly every half-hour for eight or ten hours, then dry the leg well and bathe with a solution of CURINE diluted with five times equal quantities water and alcohol. Give ten to twenty drops each, fluid extract aconite and digitalis every two hours until fever is reduced. If at the end of a week or so some enlargement still remains, paint with CURINE diluted with equal quantities water and alcohol twice daily for two weeks. Wash thoroughly every other day with warm water and soap and when dry apply the CURINE.

INDIGESTION.

The cause of indigestion is found to vary in different horses. The seat of the trouble is mostly in the stomach or small intestines, and may be caused by bad teeth, bolting of the food, irregular feeding, or wintering on bulky food, such as cornstalks, bad hay, etc.

SYMPTOMS.—Irregular and depraved appetite; bowels irregular; refusing food at times, and at others eating ravenously; skin very hard and hide bound.

FROM THE HOME OF QUARTERMASTER, 2:21¼.

Danbury, Conn., June 28, 1897.

H. S. Bossart & Co., Latrobe, Pa.

Gentlemen:—Please send us one-half dozen bottles Curine. We have been using this remedy for the past year with the very best of success.

Yours truly, RUNDLE & WHITE.

TREATMENT.—See that the food is of the right kind and that he is fed regularly. If the teeth are in bad shape, have them attended to at once. Give the following: **Nux** vomica, one ounce; sulphate of iron, one ounce; gentian, two ounces. Mix and divide into twenty-one powders and give one in his feed each meal.

CHAFING.

These wounds are caused by the chafing of the harness, collar or saddle, and are most common in the spring of the year, when the animal's skin is tender. The harness and collars should be well cleaned and oiled before the spring work is to be commenced, and see that your harness and collar fit the animal in the proper way, as ill-fitting collars, in particular, are apt to cause sore shoulders at any time. After the work for the day is done, bathe the shoulders and the back where the saddle rests well with cold water, and should you wish the skin to become tough, bathe with a solution of white-oak bark.

TREATMENT.—This is very simple if the cause be removed at once. Wash well with warm water and soap, then paint over the surface twice daily with CURINE diluted with ten times equal quantities of water and alcohol, until a cure is effected.

WOUNDS—PUNCTURED.

Punctured wounds are much more common than any other wounds of the horse, and are produced by a blunt or sharp substance, such as the puncture of a fork or nails, etc. These wounds most frequently happen to the legs and feet and should have prompt attention. The puncture of the foot is the most serious and may be caused by stepping on a nail or pieces of iron; or in shoeing, a nail may be driven too near or into the quick. If the nail be removed at once he may not show any lameness at the present time, but, **unless properly** attended to, he may become very lame in a day or two. If the nail remains in the foot the animal will become worse from the start, until the cause is removed and proper attention given to it. If a smith should drive a nail too close to the quick, lameness may not make its appearance for a week or more.

TREATMENT.—The pain from wounds in the feet are very severe; the animal will raise and lower the limb and the tendons and the fetlock may swell. Have the shoe removed at once; draw the nails separately, and notice if there is any matter in the nail holes; if not, examine the nails for moisture. If no indication of trouble is revealed, pinch or tap the foot carefully, and if pain is indicated at any special point, pare the sole down thin and when the proper place is located cut through the sole at this spot. Remove all the sole that has been undermined with pus. Poultice the foot for a couple of days with linseed meal and then insert in cavity a plug of oakum or cotton saturated with CURINE once daily until cure is effected. Apply roller bandage around foot if necessary. The horse should be shod with a leather sole under shoe packed with cotton or oakum, to keep dirt from entering the wound.

SORE THROAT.

Inflammation of the larynx is a serious disease and is usually complicated with inflammation of the pharynx and is commonly called sore throat.

SYMPTOMS.—The first symptoms noticed is a difficulty in swallowing, followed by a cough. The

---

WORTH ITS WEIGHT IN GOLD.
                    Indianapolis, Ind., Dec. 6, 1895.
H. S. Bossart & Co.
  Gentlemen:—We have given your Curine a thorough trial in our stable, and must say that its work surpasses that of any other absorbent we have used. It is worth its weight in gold when used on a valuable horse.
            FRANK STARR, W. H. BOYCE,
                Owners of Brightlight, 2:08¼.

mouth becomes hot and the glands swollen; membrane in the nostrils becomes a reddish color and a discharge soon appears.

TREATMENT.—Place the animal in a comfortable stall. Blanket the body and apply dry bandages on the legs. Place a small handful of hay in a bucket and pour a pail full of boiling water over it. Hold the animal's head over the pail and let him inhale the steam for fifteen minutes; keep stirring with a wisp of hay in order to cause the steam to raise more freely. Repeat every hour until relieved. Rub the throat, from ear to ear, well with CURINE, twice a day for three or four days. His diet should be of a laxative order, but should constipation exist, give him an injection of warm water every six hours for a day or two. Keep a pail full of cold water before him all the time, on a level with his head, so that he will not inflict pain by raising or lowering his head. Should suffocation seem inevitable, call in a qualified veterinary and have him perform tracheotomy.

For swollen or suppurated glands always use CURINE. Paint twice a day until cure is effected.

SIDE BONES.

A sidebone is the transformation of the lateral cartilages found on the wings of the coffin bone into bony matter by the deposition of lime salts. The disease is common among all kinds of horses. They mostly appear in the front feet and are of a slow growth. They cause lameness when developed. They may be caused by injuries of the cartilages, or from the weight of the animal.

TREATMENT.—If feverish and sore, apply cold water bandages for a couple of days until the inflammation has disappeared, then paint thoroughly with CURINE, two or three times a day for a week. If, upon returning to work, the trouble reappears, repeat the treatment.

SPRAINS.

When sprains occur in the legs, apply cold water bandages until fever is reduced, and then paint with CURINE twice daily until cure is effected.

When in the shoulder, bathe thoroughly and paint with CURINE twice a day until relieved. Let the animal rest for a week.

ABSCESSES.

Abscesses may be caused by bad fitting collars, colds, distemper, inflammation in the glands or muscular tissue. At first the swelling is hard, but in a little while it becomes soft, mostly in the center.

TREATMENT.—If they are slow in coming to a head, paint over the affected part twice a day with CURINE. When they come to a head, open them at the softest spot and squeeze the pus out gently. Sponge it thoroughly with warm water a couple of times a day and keep the wound open for two or three days. Inject ten to fifteen drops of CURINE once daily, diluted with four times water.

PLEURISY.

The pleura is the thin membrane that covers the lungs and the internal wall of the chest. In health the pleura throws off a fluid to prevent a friction between the lungs and the other parts which come in contact with them. When the pleura fails to throw off the fluid, there is a friction that causes

---

FROM MAJ. L. H. BEAN, THE GREAT AUCTIONEER.

Ravenna, Ohio, Feb. 10, 1896.

H. S. Bossart & Co., Latrobe, Pa.

Gentlemen:—The bottle of Curine I ordered from you did its work to perfection. For Wind Puffs and ugly sores on horses I believe it has no equal. It is indispensable in the stable of a humane horse owner.   Yours sincerely,   L. H. BEAN.

inflammation of the membrane, and we have what is called pleurisy.

SYMPTOMS.—The animal becomes sort of stiff and has no inclination to turn or move about. He may act as though he had pain; elbows and feet turned out; scarcely notice his ribs moving when breathing, as each breath causes pain. His ears and legs are cold, temperature and pulse high. If you strike the ribs in different places with your knuckles, you will come to the affected part and the animal will evince great pain, or groan. The trouble may terminate favorably in six or eight days. In some cases swelling may appear under the chest and down the legs, and if the fluid contains pus it generally proves fatal.

TREATMENT.—Place in a comfortable stall, with plenty of pure air. Blanket the body and apply dry bandages to the legs; give a laxative diet and a plentiful supply of cold water. Give from a half to a pint of raw linseed oil and apply hot fomentations to the breast. If he should show pain give two ounces tincture of opium every four hours for a day or two. From the beginning give the following drench three times a day: Solution of the acetate of ammonia, two ounces; bicarbonate of potassium, one-half ounce; spirits of nitrous ether, two ounces; water, one-half to one pint. In three or four days, when the fever and pain have somewhat subsided, rub the breast and affected side, or sides, once a day with CURINE diluted with equal quantities of water and alcohol. This will greatly promote the absorption of the effusion.

CRAMP OF THE LEG.

A cramp of the leg may be due to an irritation of the nerves of the thigh; or it may come in cold weather, and it comes sometimes after severe exercise. The leg is cold and the animal can scarcely move it. It may be of short duration and it may continue for a week.

TREATMENT.—Rub the muscles well with CURINE and repeat twice a day until they are relaxed.

HIP-LAMENESS.

Hip disease or lameness is similar in its causes and results to that of shoulder lameness, and is mostly caused by a sprain which may be brought about by overexertion, slipping, etc. It will, of course, manifest itself by signs and appearances and is more marked when the bones are diseased than when the muscles are affected. In examining for hip joint disease, the lame side will be found to be fuller, more developed and warmer. Grasp the foot and produce a passive motion, and when the foot is dropped to the ground it will produce pain. If the animal is moved along at a fair gait the trouble will also be noticeable.

TREATMENT.—Give the horse rest and paint with Dr. Turnbull's CURINE over the affected part twice a day for one week, or until a cure is effected. In hip lameness the CURINE can be used more freely as the seat of the lameness is very deep.

SCOURS—DIARRHEA.

Horses that have long legs, and long and flat bodies, are more subject to diarrhea than those of a blocky build, and more especially if fed and watered immediately before driving, although any animal is liable to scours from many different causes, such as an inflammatory condition of the intestinal canal or its annexed organs; or it may be due from eating musty food, bad condition of the teeth, impure water, etc.

TREATMENT.—The first thing to look after is the kind of water and food he has been getting, and if either of these are at fault discontinue them at once. If it results from some irritant in the intestines, give a pint of raw linseed oil and the diar-

---

When you ask your dealer for Dr. Turnbull's CURINE, see that you get the genuine. The signature of W. A. W. Turnbull, V. M. D., will be found upon the wrapper on every bottle of CURINE.

rhea will mostly disappear after the operation of the oil ceases; but should the purging continue, it can be easily checked by giving buckwheat or wheat flour in water; or two ounces of laudanum; or two ounces of paregoric three times a day. Afterwards feed a laxative diet for a few days.

TOE AND QUARTER CRACKS.

Toe cracks nearly always affect the hind feet, while quarter cracks are most common in the fore feet, and appear on the lateral parts of the wall. Toe cracks may appear on any part of the wall, but ordinarily they are seen directly in front. They may involve only the outer portion of the wall, or they may be deep and involve the whole wall and tissues beneath.

CAUSE.—Heavy shoes with nails set too far back toward the heel, fast work on hard track or road that is dry; excessive dryness of the hoof; bruises and calk wounds are also causes of quarter cracks.

SYMPTOMS.—The fissure of the horn is very often the only evidence of the disease, and this is sometimes hidden by the long hair on the coronet, or it may be filled in with putty, wax or mud. They sometimes commence on the inside of the wall and leave a very thin layer on the outside surface.

In quarter cracks, when the foot receives the

PROMINENT ATTORNEY AND PROPRIETOR OF LYKENS VALLEY FARM.

Lykens, Pa., Dec. 31, 1895.
H. S. Bossart & Co., Latrobe, Pa.

Gentlemen:—Your Curine is the best absorbent I ever used. Within the last two months I removed two very bad Curbs, one Splint, cured the worst set of tendons I ever saw, and is having magic effect on a horse that has a severe case of Navicular Disease. In the last mentioned case I have only been using it two weeks, but I expect a permanent cure. Enclosed find a check for one-half dozen more bottles. Yours truly,

EX-SENATOR A. F. THOMPSON.

weight of the body, the fissure closes, while in toe cracks it opens.

The lameness of sand cracks is slight when the animal walks, but on hard roads the faster he is made to trot the worse he limps.

TREATMENT.—In ordinary cases of quarter crack, shoe with a tip. Stimulate the growth of the horn by painting around the coronet twice daily with CURINE for two or three days, and then turn to pasture for a couple of weeks, when he may be taken up and shod with a bar shoe and put to work.

In toe cracks, lower the heel by paring, but spare the toe, except directly under the crack, where it is to be pared away until it rests free from the shoe. The shoe should have a clip on each side of the fissure. Paint the coronary band with CURINE same as for quarter cracks.

If the above treatment fails, the horn must be softened by the use of warm water and poultices and the walls of the fissure removed with the knife in the shape of the letter V. Sponge the wound thoroughly with the following solution: CURINE, one part; water, ten parts. Now saturate a pad of oakum with the same solution; place it over the wound and bandage with a damp roller bandage. Repeat once a day for a week, and then the oakum and bandage only will be needed.

GLANDERS—FARCY.

Glanders and farcy are the same disease, only the first term applies to the disease when the lesions occur in the internal organs; and the second term is applied to it when the lesions appear on the skin of the animal. It is a fatal disease, sooner or later. We read of it in ancient history as affecting the army of Constantine as far back as B. C. 330, and some of the veterinarians in those early days gave a very good description of this terrible disease. It is very contagious and may be readily communicated to the human race. Horned cattle are about the only class of animals exempt from this disease. Glanders is characterized by the formation of tubercles which degenerate into ulcers from which exudes a discharge that contains virus, and, if inoculated, will destroy the entire system.

TREATMENT.—So far as medicine is concerned, there is no drug that would be of any benefit to this disease. We would advise that the owner on first suspicion of glanders, destroy the animal immediately, and all articles with which he has come in contact should be disinfected at once. The laws of the different states are very stringent in regard to animals being affected with glanders, and should the owner try to hide the presence of the disease he should be punished to the full extent of the law.

SPRAINS OF THE LOINS.

This affection is difficult to distinguish from many similar cases. The muscles of the back and loin are injured.

SYMPTOMS.—If the animal yields or shrinks from pressure or pinching on the back near the loin, he is pronounced by many as having kidney trouble or sprained in the loins. This is mostly an error, as the majority of horses, and especially high-bred animals, will yield from a slight pressure when in the best of health. If the back or loins

---

FROM A MERCHANT AND VERY PROMINENT HORSEMAN IN CANADA.

Sherbrooke, P. Q., Jan. 23, 1896.

H. S. Bossart & Co., Latrobe, Pa.

Gentlemen:—I have removed three Ringbones from a 3-year-old colt, one of which was an extremely large and hard one; also a bad Curb from a 3-year-old pacing colt, and some very bad Wind Puffs from my 5-year-old pacing gelding, record 2:26¼, and he can beat 2:15. He is now as sound as a new milled dollar, since I have used your Curine on him. Yours truly,

SETH C. NUTTER.

be sprained, the animal will yield from pressure of any kind, and while at rest he will stand with his back in an arched condition and hind legs separated, or if in motion and is made to stop suddenly he will evince pain and probably throw his hind legs forward under the body.

TREATMENT.—Give the animal rest, and, if possible, place him in a sling. Bathe the back and over the loins well with hot water, and when dry paint with CURINE diluted with equal parts alcohol and water. Repeat twice a day for four or five days, and allow the animal rest for another week.

CANKER.

Canker of the foot is a disease produced by a vegetable parasite. It destroys the sole, frog, and sets up inflammation in the deeper tissues. The parasite may be called contagious, but they must find a suitable place in the foot to grow before they are reproduced. Dampness is the most favorable cause for the development of this disease, as it is much more common in wet than in dry seasons.

SYMPTOMS.—It may appear in all the feet at the same time, but usually it will be found in one foot and then in the other, etc. When it attacks the foot you will notice a thin watery discharge, and as this secretion dries it forms a matter very offensive to the sense of smell, and later will rot away the horn of the frog, and sole, and when this is destroyed lameness will appear.

TREATMENT.—Cleanse the foot thoroughly with warm water and apply a linseed poultice containing

---

HOME OF THE LATE AMBASSADOR, 2:21¼.

Kalamazoo, Mich., Feb. 8, 1896.

H. S. Bossart & Co., Latrobe, Pa.

Gentlemen:—We have been using your Curine for the past six months with the best of success. It has no superior for deep-seated troubles, and we cheerfully recommend it. Very truly yours,

THE KALAMAZOO FARM CO.

one-half to one ounce of CURINE; when well poulticed, remove all the diseased portions of the horn; cut off all the prominent points of the soft tissues and nail on carefully a broad plain shoe. Now paint with CURINE over the diseased portion; place a pad of oakum over the foot and apply a roller bandage. Repeat once a day until the soft tissues are all horned over, then dilute CURINE with five times water and continue the dressing until a permanent cure is effected. Do not allow your patience to become exhausted in treating for canker, as in some cases it is very slow to yield.

CONTRACTED HEELS.

Contracted heels is a disease common among horses that are kept on hard dry floors. It nearly always affects the fore feet, and is caused by the tissues of the foot shrinking away, which may be the result of too sudden a change from wet, marshy ground to dry stables; or faulty shoeing. They may also become contracted from diseases, such as ringbone, navicular disease, corns, thrush, canker. etc.

SYMPTOMS.—The whole hoof is so dry and hard that it can scarcely be cut; the heels are higher; the frog is pinched and much shrunken between the enclosing heels. When the disease is advanced, lameness will appear.

TREATMENT.—Remove the shoe and lower the heels; soak the foot or feet in cold water with a handful of salt in it for a couple of days until the horn becomes soft; or, if desired, the foot may be poulticed until the horn is soft. Now shoe with a

BEST IN THE WORLD.

Read what Dick Wilson, of Binghamton, N. Y., driver of Bumps, 2:04¾, and other good ones, says: "I have been using Curine for the last three months and I am free to say that I think it the best preparation in the world. It will reach deep-seated troubles where all other medicines fail. I find the same verdict among all first-class drivers and owners at the Buffalo meeting."

"tip," rasp away the horn of the wall until a thin layer covers the tissues beneath the heel so that the frog may rest on the ground. Paint around the coronet with CURINE once a day for a week and repeat in three or four weeks. This will stimulate a rapid and healthy growth of horn. If the animal's service can be spared, turn him to pasture in a damp field for a month or so; if not, use some good hoof ointment on the horn and sole and make the floor of his stall damp with clay or wet straw. If all horses stood on damp clay floors there would be few contracted heels.

SPRAINS OF THE FETLOCK.

Sprains of the fetlock mostly happen to the fore leg, and trotters, pacers and runners are particularly liable to this injury.

CAUSES.—It generally happens by making a misstep, slipping, stumbling, or the animal is caught in a rut or hole and struggles violently.

SYMPTOMS.—While at rest the leg is flexed at the joint affected and the toe rests on the ground. The joint swells and becomes hot.

TREATMENT.—Give the animal rest and apply cold water bandages every hour until the fever has subsided, then paint with Dr. Turnbull's CURINE twice daily for one week; allow the animal another

---

CURINE CURES.

Buffalo, N. Y., July 1, 1895.

H. S. Bossart & Co., Latrobe, Pa.:

In April I purchased a bottle of your Curine. Since that time I have thoroughly tested the merits of this medicine, and I am free to say that I have never used anything that would compare with it as a remedy for removing bunches of all kinds from horses. I have one horse at present that had a very bad curb that it has completely cured.

C. R. BENTLY.

Late Supt. and Mgr. Dreamland Stock Farm, Le Roy, N. Y.

week's rest, and if the lameness has not all disappeared, repeat the treatment with the CURINE. If the ligaments of the joint are ruptured the lameness may last quite a while.

FROG BRUISE.

A bruise of the frog usually happens from the animal stepping on a hard object. If a stone is wedged between the sides of the frog, or in the cleft of the frog, and allowed to remain there for some time it may produce the same result, especially if he is moving at a fast gait.

SYMPTOMS.—When the animal moves, the toe is placed to the ground, and when he is resting the leg is extended, with the toe resting on the ground. This is done in order to keep all pressure from the frog. When the injured spot is found and no opening exists, it should be pared through until a thin watery pus escapes; if a ragged opening exists and a greenish pus is escaping, gangrene of the plantar cushion has set in.

TREATMENT.—Remove the shoe, pare the sole down thin and poultice the foot for a couple of days. When the pus has loosened the horn, all the detached portions should be cut away. If gangrene of the plantar cushion has set in, one-half of the frog, or probably the whole of it, will be found to have separated from the plantar cushion and should be removed with the knife. In a couple of days the unhealthy portion of the cushion will slough off from the effects of the poultice. Now take a camel's hair brush and pencil the wound

---

FROM THE OWNER OF HUSTLER RUSSELL, 2:12½.

Tarentum, Pa., Feb. 11, 1896.

H. S. Bossart & Co., Latrobe, Pa.

Gentlemen:—I have used your Curine and think it has no equal for all kinds of bony enlargements, sprains and other ailments. Very truly,

H. A. MOORHEAD, Owner and Trainer.

with a solution of one part CURINE to four parts water; cover the wound carefully with a pad of oakum saturated in the same solution, and apply a roller bandage. Repeat once a day until a thin layer of new horn has grown over the exposed parts. The animal may now be shod, first cover the frog with a pad of oakum held in place by a piece of leather covering the foot and nailed on with the shoe. Give slow work for a couple of weeks.

DISTEMPER.

Distemper appears as a fever and lasts for a few days, with formation of matter in the lungs and air tubes, which may form abscesses in various parts of the body. It is an infectious disease, but it generally leaves the animal in as healthy a form as before, and also from future trouble of the same kind.

CAUSES.—Young horses from one to five years of age are more subject to this disease than older animals, and as it is infectious, it is very often brought about by the colt being placed in a stable with older horses that may be bearers of some infectious disease. Standard and thoroughbred horses are more apt to contract the disease at an earlier age than heavier or more sluggish animals.

SYMPTOMS.—The coat becomes dry, the hair stands on end, appetite may or may not be diminished; horse may have chills in different parts of the body, fever, and pulse becomes high; eyes and mouth are of a reddish color. The colt may sneeze and cough, and at the end of a couple of days a thin watery discharge from the nostrils takes place, and later it becomes thicker and of a yellowish color. In a couple of days after the discharge has taken place you will notice a swelling under the jaw which will gradually form an abscess, break open and discharge. At the end of four or five days the discharge lessens; the animal regains his appetite and is himself again.

TREATMENT.—Protect him from the cold and make him comfortable with blankets. If his appetite remains good, feed him good clean hay, oats and a nice hot bran mash once or twice a day. If the fever is high, feed him a small handful of Epsom salts twice a day. Put a small handful of hay with a little pine tar on it in a bucket and pour a pail of boiling water over it; hold the horse's head over this for ten or fifteen minutes and let him inhale the steam thoroughly; keep stirring it with a wisp of hay. Repeat three or four times a day until the cough is relieved. If the abscess under the jaw is large, open it at once and bathe it and the swollen gland well with warm water. Do not blister the throat, as no medicine is necessary for the treatment of distemper, unless other complications arise.

MANGE.

Mange is due to the irritation of the skin caused by a small parasite.

SYMPTOMS.—An incessant and increasing itching in some parts of the back, mane, head, tail and lower parts of the legs or heels. The hair may be rubbed off, eruptions and scab formed from the effects of the constant scratching.

TREATMENT.—Wash thoroughly with warm water and castile soap until scabs are removed, and when dry paint over the affected parts with CURINE. Repeat once a day for two or three days. Wash all harness, brushes, curry combs and stable utensils in a solution of creolol, two ounces to one gallon of water. Boil all blankets and rubbing cloths in water and whitewash the stalls. As a new family of these parasites are raised about every two weeks, it would be well at the end of that time to apply CURINE again for a couple of days, same as before.

MASTURBATION—SELF-ABUSE.

Stallions acquire this vicious habit, stimulating the sexual instinct to the discharge of semen by rubbing the penis against the belly. This habit is very common among standard and thoroughbred stallions. The writer has seen high-bred colts one year old abuse themselves, and very often when young colts at the age of one and two years do not thrive, the direct cause can be traced to self-abuse.

TREATMENT.—Always keep a stallion shield on your horse; plenty of good ones on the market, such as the Tenny, Springsteen, Kentucky, etc. A stallion that is not worth a shield is not worth having.

FROM MORNINGSIDE FARM.

Morningside Farm, Ligonier, Pa., May 9, 1896.
H. S. Bossart & Co., Latrobe, Pa.

Gentlemen:—We have used "Curine" for enlargements and callous lumps on several horses with most satisfactory results in every case.

H. S. DENNY & BROS.,
Owners of Grosjean, 2:24¾; Forest Wilkes, 2:14¼.

SHOEING.

Although the subject discussed in the present chapter may not be entitled to a place in a category of the ailments to which horseflesh is heir, bad and indifferent shoeing are such prolific sources of both disability and disease in the noblest of all our dumb animals, that no excuse is necessary in claiming for it equal attention at the hands of those interested. No horseman questions the old saying "no foot, no horse," and yet in no portion of that animal's economy has he suffered so many wrongs as in his feet, which is due directly or indirectly to improper shoeing. We are reluctant to admit that the ordinary iron or steel shoe is the best artificial protection to the horse's foot. That the system of horseshoeing as it obtains even in the most skillful hands, is pregnant with mischief to the foot, no one who is conversant with the facts will deny. Each time a horse is shod—every nail drawn—means so much injury to the foot. The better the job the less injury.

We have, however, to deal with the facts as we find them, and as we have to impose upon our horse's work of a nature that entails upon their feet more waste of horn than nature can replace during the ordinary interval of rest, we are obliged to adopt a defense of some kind.

Without wishing to do injustice to the rural knights of the anvil, it is nevertheless a lamentable truth that these votaries of the buttress and drawing-knife are, all the world over, so wedded to a number of traditionary practices, so heinous and prejudicial to the interest of the horse and his owner that one might well be excused for wondering whether their mission were not to mar instead of to protect the perfect handiwork of our Creator.

Ignorant at the anatomy and physiology of the parts, they cut, they mutilate and carve as whim, prejudice or time-honored custom dictates. Disaster it may be slowly, but surely follows and the poor dumb creatures' suffering foots the bill. Let us glance at some of the traditional practices.

Among them is the insane habit of trimming the frog and thinning out the sole till it will visibly yield to the pressure of the operators' thumbs. The frog is nature's cushion and hoof-expander, placed there by an all-wise hand; by its elasticy it wards off concussion from the less elastic portion of the structure and by its resilence assists in maintaining the natural expansion of its horny ambit, that is, it does so in its natural state, but the drawing-knife touch is fatal to it. Once cut, carved and deprived of its pressure, causes it to shrink, dry, and harden and at once lose those attributes which constitutes its usefulness to the foot.

The operator next turns his attention to the sole, which, by all traditions of the craft, must be pared down until only a thin, soft and partially formed horn is left to protect the living structures within against injury from the substances from which the foot necessarily comes in contact with.

On this maimed foot a shoe, often many sizes too small, is tacked, and the rasp is mostly used to reduce the foot to fit the shoe; for although it is apparently of little moment whether the shoe fits the foot, but it is necessary that the foot, somehow or other, fit the shoe. The foot is now shod and protected from undue wear, to be sure, but at what a sacrifice! Robbed of its cushion, its natural expander; its sole mangled; its horny wall crushed and deflected by an unncessary number of nails; robbed by the rasp of its cortical layer of natural varnish, which retains the moisture secreted by the economy, and the foot is a very sorry plight indeed. It is a fact all the world over the farrier is the only one among all our artisans who is least amenable to suggestions from his employer. When the ordinary horse-owner takes his animal to the shoeing forge he has usually to place himself in the blacksmith's hands and give him his own way to cut and carve at his unholy will, or else take his horse elsewhere and then probably find himself no better off. The result is that his horse's feet are mercilessly mutilated instead of being left as nearly as possible as nature made them.

THE SHOE.

The shoe should be as light as the weight of the animal and the nature of the work he is expected to perform will admit of.

The mission of the shoe is to prevent undue wear of the walls, and a light shoe will do this as well as a heavy one. Make the shoe to fit the foot instead of the foot to fit the shoe. Level the foot perfectly and use the knife very sparingly and do not cut away any of the frog as nature will take care of that. Use small nails and not too many; do not drive too high up into the walls. If a perfectly level bearing has been obtained—as ought to be the case—it is astonishing how few and how small nails will hold the shoe firmly in its place. When the shoe has been fitted, the nails drawn up and clinched, there should be nothing left to be done. It is just at this stage that the incompetent workman, in the most uncalled for manner, inflicts serious and lasting injuries on the foot by rasping away the thin coating of natural varnish on the outer portion of the foot which is put there by nature to protect the moisture necessary for the protection of the horn and foot.

Shoes should be removed, refitted and redriven every four to six weeks.

In this short article on shoeing we are not writing for the trotting horseman who knows his own business better than we can teach him, and thanks be to him for the amount of attention that he has given to proper shoeing which tends to the more perfect development of that paragon of horse-flesh, the American trotter, who has made better progress in America than in any other country on the face of the globe.

The different styles of shoes which have been devised are marvels of ingenuity, and many of them are admirably effective as remedial agents for faulty gaits and uneven action. Their number is infinite, but as many of them are applicable only to horses used solely for speed purposes, an attempt to give a description would be out of place in a work of this kind.

I will guarantee my CURINE to be the most powerful paint that medical science can formulate. It will reach DEEPER-SEATED TROUBLES and produce better effects for LAMENESS and unhealthy sores than any other preparation in the world, for which local medication is indicated, such as Spavins, Curbs, Splints, Ringbones, Sprung Knees, Rheumatism, Lameness of all kinds, Soft Bunches, Bony Growths, etc.

None genuine without my signature on labels. W A. W. TURNBULL, V. M. D., late House Surgeon, Veterinary Hospital, University of Pennsylvania.

CURINE is the most powerful paint known, and supersedes all cautery or firing. It contains no grease and will not blemish or remove the hair.

Its effects are absorbent, alterative, penetrative, and antiseptic, and will reach the deepest-seated troubles. Horses can be worked as usual while using this marvelous paint. It is used with phenomenal success in all the leading stables. WE WILL WAGER $100 that it will produce better effects for the same curatives than any other compound in the world.

WE GUARANTEE that one bottle of CURINE will produce better results than any other paint, liniment or spavin cure ever made. EVERY BOTTLE OF CURINE is sold warranted to give satisfaction. It is recommended by such owners as Allen Farm, C. H. Nelson, E. W. Ayers, M. Salisbury, M. B. Laird, J. G. Taylor, C. W. Williams, Calumet Stock Farm, Forbes Farm, Rundle & White, and by drivers such as Chas. Marvin. John Splan, Andy McDowell, Budd Doble, Geo. Starr, Jack Curry, John Kelly, John Dickerson, Scott Quintin, Wm. Andrews, Knap McCarthy, and thousands of others.

Sole Manufacturers:

H. S. BOSSART & CO.,
Latrobe, Pa., U. S. A.

Price—Large bottles, $2.00; Small bottles, $1.00.

DR. TURNBULL'S PREPARATION FROM A SCIENTIFIC STANDPOINT.

Clipping from the Western Horseman, May 16, appearing also in Chicago Horseman, May 23; Kentucky Stock Farm, May 23; American Sportsman, May 23; Horse Review, May 28; Turf, Field and Farm, May 30, 1895:

Of the many proprietary and quack medicines now on the market very few have any medicinal value. The proprietors of most veterinary preparations know absolutely nothing of veterinary science, equally little of the action of compounding of drugs, and having no reputation at stake, rely on extensive advertising, a few bogus testimonials and considerable gall in order to sell their nostrums. Again, the low figure at which many of these are placed on the market is in itself prima facie evidence of fraud. Some time ago the firm of H. S. Bossart & Co. commenced advertising a preparation formulated by Dr. Turnbull. These gentlemen claim great curative powers for their medicine, and they are responsible people. I determined to put their preparation to the same thorough test, both practical and analytical, to which I have subjected many other proprietary mixtures, and to give the results to the horse-loving public. During the time taken up by my investigation (in which I was greatly assisted by a medical friend) I procured more information about the members of the firm, visited their excellent laboratory and interviewed many of the most prominent horsemen who have used their preparation. Dr. Turnbull, the originator of the formulas, is an experienced and well-known veterinarian. The doctor is a graduate of the University of Pennsylvania, and he also studied in Europe. At the University of Pennsylvania he not only held a position in the Veterinary School, but was also resident surgeon in the veterinary hospital attached to that institution. This hospital is the finest in the country, and its free clinics, etc., give exceptional facilities for study. Not satisfied with his own opinion, Dr. Turnbull made several trips to Europe to consult the most prominent veterinary scientists in regard to his preparation, which, after repeated and careful trials on the most hopeless cases, he then placed on the market. Mr. H. S. Bossart, the manufacturer, is a prominent business man and proprietor of the fine new driving park at Latrobe. Mr. Bossart recognized the need of such a medicine, and, having often seen the grand results from Dr. Turnbull's treatment, became interested in the business.

From the above it is easily seen that a guarantee from such men should convey great weight. Of the above preparations I cannot speak too highly, and from the chemist's standpoint it is a model of the highest excellence.

After repeated trials by myself and assistant they have accomplished what the manufacturers claim for it, and any horseman who is in need of such medicine will serve his own and animal's interest by using Dr. Turnbull's medicine.

A QUALIFIED VETERINARY.

REFERENCES.

F. & T. E. Drake, Lebanon, Ohio, owner of Moquette, 2:10.

C. W. Williams, Galesburg, Ill., owner of Allerton, 2:09¼.

H. Y. Haws, Johnstown, Pa., owner of Chance, 2:12¼.

Ethanmont Farm, Washington, Pa., owner of Happy Wanderer, 2:20½.

Matt. H. Laird, Mansfield, O., owner of Reubenstein, 2:05.

Morris J. Jones, Red Oak, Ia., owner of Alix, 2:03¾.

Lewis & Albaugh, Circleville, O., owner of Wilton, 2:19¼.

F. P. Doble, Elyria, O., trainer at Elyria Stock Farm.

F. J. Keys, Cleveland, O., trainer at Forest City Farm.

J. C. Collins, Supt. Meadow Lands Farm, driver of Raven, 2:10¼.

Sutherland & Benjamin, Saginaw, Mich., owners of Spinx, 2:20½.

Walter Clark, Battle Creek, Mich., former owner of Pilot Medium.

Lesh Stock Farm, Goshen, Ind., owner of Online, 2:04.

Centliver Bros., Fort Wayne, Ind., owners of Atlantic King, 2:09¼.

Ross & Dickenson, Madison, Ind., owners of Mikagan, 2:19¾.

Keystone Stock Farm, Omaha, Neb., owner of The Conqueror, 2:12¼.

W. A. Jones & Son, Rushville, Ind., owners of Ravan Wilkes, 2:15½.

Rumberger Live Stock Co., Indianapolis, Ind., former owner of Will Kerr, 2:07½.

D. W. Brennmean & Bro., Decatur, Ill., owners of Effie Powers, 2:10½.

Daniel Sapp, Pekin, Ill., owner of Billie Wilkes.

Railey Bros., Versailles, Ky., breeders of fine carriage and saddle horses.

Robert Aull, St. Louis, Mo.

A. J. Haws, Johnstown, Pa., owner of Alhambra, 2:08¼.

Fairview Stock Farm, Kewanna, Ind.

M. Moses, Baltimore, Md., supplies city with horses.

A. L. McCrea, Gouverneur, N. Y., Patron Farm.

Wm. Simpson, New York City, owner of Empire City Stud.

W. J. White, Rockport, O., owner of 2-Minute Stock Farm.

Simmocolon Stock Farm, Detroit, Mich., owner of Sidney, 2:19¼.

Powell Bros., Shadeland Stock Farm, Shadeland, Pa.

Kalamazoo Farm Co., Kalamazoo, Mich., owners of Ambassador, 2:21¾.

Allen Farm, Pittsfield, Mass., owner of Kremlin, 2:07¾.

Arden Farm, Goshen, N. Y., owner of Stamboul, 2:07½.

John H. Shultz, Brooklyn, N. Y., Parkville Farm.

W. B. Fasig, Cleveland, O.

Alamance Stock Farm, Graham, N. C., former owners of John R. Gentry, 2:00½.

W. C. France & Son, New York City, owners of Red Wilkes.

J. E. Thayer & Bro., Lancaster, Mass., owners of Allandorf, 2:19½.

Calumet Stock Farm, Chicago, Ill., owners of Roy Wilkes, 2:06½.

Village Farm, East Aurora, N. Y., former owner of Robert J., 2:01½.

Robert Bonner, Tarrytown, N. Y., owner of Maud S., 2:08¾.

W. T. Campbell, Baltimore, Md., driver of Lena Hill (2), 2:12¾.

John G. Taylor, Chebanse, Ill., former owner of Joe Patchen, 2.01¼.

DuBois Bros., Denver, Col., owners of Carbonate, (2) 2:09.

John Spian, Glenville, O., trainer.

Denny Bros., Ligonier, Pa., owners of Grossjean, 2:24¾.

Forbes Farm, Ponkapog, Mass., owner of Arion, 2:07¾.

Wm. M. Hill, Dallas, Tex., owner of Wm. M. Hill, 2:20.

C. H. Nelson, Waterville, Me., owner of Nelson, 2:09.

Geo. H. Ketcham, Toledo, O., owner of Robert McGregor, 2:17½.

Monroe Salisbury, Pleasanton, Cal., former owner of Azote, 2:04¾.

A. C. Pennock, Cleveland, O., owner and trainer.

Maj. L. H. Bean, Ravenna, O., stock auctioneer.

G. A. Goodrich, Shelbyville, Ind., former owner of Angie D., 2.07.

Bowerman Bros., Lexington, Ky., owners and trainers.

Frost Stock Farm, Roodhouse, Ill., owner of Bonnie McGregor, 2:13½.

Gill Curry, Lexington, Ky., owner and trainer.

Frank H. Smith, Buffalo, N. Y., professional starting judge.

Also thousands of other prominent horsemen which space will not allow us to name.

SELLING AGENTS.

Below will be found the addresses and names, in alphabetical form, of the leading druggists and turf goods houses (wholesale and retail) and a few others who sell CURINE. The wholesale trade also furnish it to the trade when requested. It can be bought in any city and nearly every town in the United States.

Correspondence solicited by the manufacturers.

ARKANSAS.

Little Rock ....Arkansas Stables.

CALIFORNIA.

Los Angeles ....F. W. Braun & Co.W. Drugs.
San Francisco ....Redington & Co...W. Drugs.
San Francisco ....J. O'Kane ....Harness.
Stockton ....Wm. A. Cowdery..Druggist.

COLORADO.

Denver ....W. A. Hover..Whol. Drugs.
Pueblo ....Reiss Bros. ....Druggists.

CONNECTICUT.

Danbury ....A. G. Cole & Co.....Harness.
Gaylordsville ....M. L. Hungerford....Agent.
Meriden ....Meriden Drug Co.............
New Haven ....C. S. Leete & Co..Druggists.
Norwich ....N. D. Sevin & Son..Drug'ts.
Rockville ....Jas. T. Fitton......Druggist.
Waterbury ....H. W. Lake.........Druggist.
Willimantic ....John T. Baker .....Druggist.

DELAWARE.

Wilmington ....Z. James Belt......Druggist.

DISTRICT OF COLUMBIA.

Washington ....Lutz Bros. ....Harness.

GEORGIA.

Griffin ....Carlisle & Ward..Druggists.
Macon ....H. J. Lamar & Sons..W. Dr.
Rome ....David W. Curry..W. Drugs.
Savannah ....Solomons & Co....Druggists.
Thomasville ....Bondurant & Peacock.Dr'ts.

ILLINOIS.

Aurora ....Rollins & Rice....Druggists.
Belvidere ....John C. Foote......Druggist.
Bloomington ....Funk & Chewning...Dr'g'ts.
Champaigne ....Watson Faulkner..Druggist.
Charleston ....A. J. Glick......Blacksmith.
Chicago ....Morrisson, Plummer & Co...
 ....Wh. Druggists.
Chicago ....Fuller & Fuller Co...W. Dr.
Chicago ....Lord, Owen & Co..W. Drugs.
Chicago ....Peter Van Schaack & Sons..
 ....Whol. Drugs.
Chicago ....Hartford & Hall....Harness.
Clinton ....J. W. Day & Son....Drug'ts.
Danville ....W. F. Baum.......Druggist.
Decatur ....W. F. Neisler Dr. & Sup. Co.
Fairbury ....Wade Bros........ Druggists.
Farmer City ....E. B. Garver & Son..Dr'g'ts.
Jerseyville ....W. S. Pittman Drug Co.......
Jerseyville ....James Dolan ....Blacksmith.
Kankakee ....J. E. Smith........Druggist.
Kewanee ....Geo. A. Anthony...Druggist.

La Harpe	J. G. Campbell	Druggist.
La Salle	R. C. Hattenhauer	Dr'g'st.
Lincoln	F. R. Pierron	Druggist.
Litchfield	F. R. Milnor	Druggist.
Monticello	F. H. Chenoweth	Druggist.
Monticello	Tinder & Hott	Druggists.
Ottawa	Wm. Hayne	Harness.
Peoria	Barker'& Wheeler Co.	W.Dr.
Princeton	W. R. Jester	Harness.
Quincy	Aldo Sommers' Drug Co.	
Roodhouse	Berry & Wolfe	Druggists.
Rushville	A. K. Smither	Druggist.
Shelbyville	L. S. & J. O. Seaman	Drgst.
Springfield	R. W. Diller	Druggist.
Waukegon	J. G. Cornish	Harness.

INDIANA.

Bloomington	Faris Bros.	Druggists.
Bluffton	Chas. C. Deam	Druggist.
Brazil	Simon Herr	Druggist.
Cambridge City	James McCaffery	Drug'st.
Cerro Gordo	J. G. Johnson	Agent.
Columbus	Hauser & Parker	Drug'ts
Connersville	A. M. Andrews	Druggist.
Crawfordsville	T. D. Brown & Son	Dr'g'ts.
Crawfordsville	C. J. Britton	V. S.
Edinburg	Compton & Maley	Harness.
Eikhart	C. H. Leonard	Druggist.
Elwood	E. E. Green & Son	Dr'g'ts.
Evansville	Chas. Leich & Co.	W. Drugs.
Fort Wayne	Meyer Bros. & Co.	W. Drugs.
Frankfort	Coulter, Given & Co.	Drgts.
Goshen	Dwight H. Hawks	Druggist.
Indianapolis	Daniel Stewart	Wh. Drugs.
Indianapolis	Indianapolis Drug Co.	W. Dr.

Indianapolis .... F. M. Rottler........Harness.
Kendallville .... Vought & Banta....Harness.
Kokomo .... Geo. E. Meck......Druggist.
Lafayette .... Harry E. Glick.....Druggist.
La Porte .... F. W. Meissner.....Druggist.
Lebanon .... Long & Staley....Druggists.
Logansport .... W. H. Bringhurst..Druggist.
Madison .... John V. Connelly.....Agent.
Marion .... Siddons Bros.......Druggists.
Mount Vernon .... W. H. Fogas........Druggist.
Muncie .... Frank B. Nickey...Druggist.
New Albany .... C. D. Knoefel......Druggist.
New Castle .... L. E. Kinsey & Co.Druggists.
New Harmony .... Wilmoth, Wilhelm & Co..Dr.
Peru .... J. E. Hendricks....Druggist.
Portland .... Isaac B. Little.....Druggist.
Richmond .... A. G. Luken & Co.W. Drugs.
Rushville .... F. B. Johnston & Co..Drgst.
Shannondale .... G. W. Shannon........Agent.
Shelbyville .... O. L. Bishop........Druggist.
South Bend .... Milton & Eliel.....Druggists.
Terre Haute .... D. P. Cox...........Druggist.
Tipton .... H. Mahlig ....Druggist.
Vincennes .... Chas. S. Miller......Druggist.
Wabash .... Sweetser & Clark...Drug'ts.
Washington .... T. H. Mitchell......Druggist.

IOWA.

Burlington .... Churchill Drug Co. ....
Cedar Rapids .... W. L. Walker......Druggist.
Clinton .... Oscar Majer ....Druggist.
Council Bluffs .... Geo. A. Davis......Druggist.
Creston .... Ed. A. Aldrich.....Druggist.
Davenport .... E. S. Ballord & Co..Drug'ts.
Davenport .... Sears-Frizzell Co. ..Saddlery.

Des Moines ....Nerman Lichty..Wh. Drugs.
Dubuque ....W. H. Torbert...Wh. Drugs.
Independence ....C. R. Wallace......Druggist.
Iowa City ....W. E. Shrader.....Druggist.
Keokuk ....D. A. Keer Drug Co..........
Le Mars ....P. H. Diehl........Druggist.
Marshalltown ....McBride & Will Drug Co....
Mason City ....Atkinson & Adams..Drug'ts.
Newton ....Foster & Callison..Gen.Store
Oskaloosa ....J. H. Pickett........Druggist.
Ottumwa ....W. R. Beck & Co...Drug'ts.
Red Oak ....Lane Imp. Co..Carr'ges, etc.
Silver City ....C. F. Mears..........Jeweler.
Sioux City ....Hornick, Hess & Moore......
............Wh. Druggists.
Waterloo ....W. W. Forry........Druggist.
Washington ....Chilcote & Cook..Druggists.
Webster City ....Arthur & Richardson..Drgst.

KANSAS.

Fort Scott ....C. E. Hall...........Druggist.
Holton ....Gus. A. Beauchamp...Drgst.
Lawrence ....Barber Bros. .....Druggists.
Leavenworth ....Adolf Lange ....Druggist.
Topeka ....Sim Drug Co. ....

KENTUCKY.

Bowling Green ....G. E. Townsend....Druggist.
Cynthiana ....J. W. Renaker.....Druggist.
Flemmingsburg ....C. H. Kehoe & Co...Drug'ts.
Georgetown............A. B. Barkley.......Harness.
Georgetown............E. Thompson ......Druggist.
Henderson ....Davis & Read....Druggists.
Lebanon ....W. F. Courts........Harness.
Lexington ....Thompson & Boyd..Harness.

Lexington ....Barkley Bros. ......Harness.
Lexington ....Davis & Robertson.Drugg'ts.
Louisville ....Robinson-Pettett Co..........
    ....Wh. Druggists.
Louisville ....Buschemeyer Bros...Dr'g'ts.
Maysville ....Keith-Schroeder Harness Co.
Mount Sterling ....W. S. Lloyd.........Druggist.
Owensboro ....Mullen & Haynes..W.&R.Dr.
Paducah ....Du Bois & Co..W.&R.Drugs.
Paris ....Clarke & Kenney..Druggists.
Richmond ....B. L. Middleton....Druggist.
Winchester ....Winchester Drug Co.........

LOUISIANA.

New Orleans ....L. N. Brunswig..Wh. Drugs.

MAINE.

Auburn ....W. A. Robinson & Co.Drg'st.
Augusta ....Bowditch, Webster & Co.Dr.
Bangor ....Caldwell Sweet ....Druggist.
Biddeford ....John Berry ....Druggist.
Bridgton ....I. S. Webb & Son....Harness.
Dover ....D. E. Larrabee...........
    ....Prop. Wilkes Farm.
Lewiston ....D. W. Wiggin & Co...Drgts.
Portland ....Cook, Everett & Pennell..
    ....Wh. Druggists.
Skowhegan ....H. W. Cushing.....Druggist.
Waterville ....C. H. Nelson..............
    ....Owner of Nelson, 2:09.

MARYLAND.

Baltimore ....Muth Bros. & Co.;W. Drugs.
Baltimore ....Lilly, Rogers & Co..;Drugs.
Cumberland ....John S. Miller......Druggist.
Hagerstown ....J. W. Cook & Bro.Druggists.

MASSACHUSETTS.

Athol	Converse & Ward	Drugg'ts.
Boston	Geo. C. Goodwin & Co.	W.Dr.
Boston	M. W. Cross & Co.	Harness.
Fall River	E. S. Anthony	Druggist.
Fall River	J. T. Touhey	Druggist.
Gloucester	A. S. Maddocks	Druggist.
Haverhill	M. F. Flynn	Druggist.
Marlborough	Burdett & Barnard	Drug'ts.
Pittsfield	R. E. Willard & Son	Drg'ts.
Springfield	New Eng. Dstbng. Co.	Agts.
Taunton	A. J. Barker	Druggist.
West Acton	Waldo Littlefield	Agent.

MICHIGAN.

Adrian	Lee B. Millard	Druggist.
Albion	Sheldon & Barber	Drug'ts.
Alpena	John T. Bostwick	Druggist.
Ann Arbor	H. J. Brown	Druggist.
Battle Creek	Amberg & Murphy	Drug'ts.
Calumet	D. T. Macdonald	Druggist.
Caro	J. J. Franklin	Harness.
Charlotte	H. A. Blackmar	Druggist.
Coldwater	E. R. Clark & Co.	Druggists.
Detroit	Williams, Davis, Brooks & Hinchman Sons	W. Dr.
Detroit	Tuttle & Clark	Harness.
Detroit	Darr Turf Goods Co.	Harn'ss.
Escanaba	Groos & Son	Druggists.
Grand Rapids	Hazeltine & Perkins Drug Co.	Whol. Drugs.
Ionia	H. Van Allen	Druggist.
Jackson	E. T. Webb	Druggist.
Kalamazoo	Kalamazoo Farm Co.	Agts.
Lansing	Alsdorf & Son	Druggists.

Ludington .... V. Roussin .... Druggist.
Manistee .... A. H. Lyman Co.. Druggists.
Marshall .... F. G. Seaman & Co.. Dr'g'ts.
Mt. Clemens .... J. H. Westendorf.. Druggist.
Muskegon .... Fred. Brundage ... Druggist.
Niles .... F. W. Richter & Co.. Dr'g'ts.
Otsego .... Richard Monteith .. Harness.
Owosso .... Johnson & Henderson.. Drg.
Paw Paw .... J. M. Longwell... Horseman.
Port Huron .... Central Drug Store...........
Saginaw .... D. E. Prall & Co.. W.&R.Dr.
St. Johns .... Travis & Baker... Druggists.
Sturgis .... D. J. Sell & Son..... Harness.
Vassar .... H. E. Harrison..... Druggist.
West Bay City......... H. H. Burdick...... Druggist.

MINNESOTA.

Fergus Falls .... Geo. C. Miles....... Druggist.
Mankato .... John C. Thro....... Druggist.
Minneapolis .... Lyman-Eliel Drug Co.W.Dr.
Minneapolis .... M. L. Burkhardt.... Harness.
New Ulm .... A. J. Eckstein...... Druggist.
St. Cloud .... J. D. McKenzie...... Trainer.
St. Paul .... Noyes Bros. & Cutler.W.Dr.
St. Paul .... Ryan Drug Co... Wh. Drugs.
Spring Grove .... T. T. Bergh.......... Harness.
Stillwater .... Theo. Jassoy & Son.Harness.
Winona .... J. W. Lauer........ Druggist.

MISSOURI.

Kansas City .... Faxon, Horton & Galla-
                            gher .... Whol. Drugs.
Kansas City .... J. J. Foster......... Harness.
St. Louis .... Moffitt-West Drug Co.W.Dr.
St. Louis .... Meyer Bros. Drug Co.. W.Dr.
St. Louis .... A. J. Hoenny....... Druggist.

Springfield ....J. W. Crank Drug Co.........
St. Joseph ....Van Natta-Lynds Drug
                           Co. ....Whol. Drugs.

MONTANA.

Anaconda ....City Drug Co. ....
Butte City ....D. M. Newbro Drug Co.W.D.
Ennis ....Jas. W. Saunders..Druggist.

NEBRASKA.

Beatrice ....J. L. Kubat.........Druggist.
Columbus ....C. E. Morse........Horseman.
Fremont ....W. J. Davies........Druggist.
Gering ....F. W. Enderly...Gen. Store.
Hastings ....G. J. Evans Drug Co..........
Lincoln ....Lincoln Drug Co..W. Drugs.
Omaha .:...............Richardson Drug Co..W. Dr.
Omaha ....E. E. Bruce & Co..W. Drugs.

NEW HAMPSHIRE.

Concord ....Eugene Sullivan Co..Dr'g'ts.
Manchester ....John B. Hall.......Druggist.
Nashua ....W. A. Lovering.....Druggist.
Rochester ....R. DeWitt Burnham.Dr'g'st.
Somersworth ....J. B. Moarne..........Agent.

NEW JERSEY.

Bridgeton ....Thos. W. Williams...Livery.
Hope ....Arthur H. Lack........Agent.
Newark ....W. H. Stanford....Druggist.
Newark ....J. E. Drummand...Saddlery.
Paterson ....C. P.Kinsilla........Druggist.
Trenton ....John S. Anistaki...Druggist.
Trenton ....Peter D. Thropp....Harness.
Westfield ....H. L. Fink..........Harness.

NEW YORK.

Albany	Walker & Gibson	W. Drugs.
Albany	Best & Stedman	W. Drugs.
Amsterdam	Powell & Wolfe	Druggists.
Auburn	The C. H. Sagar Co.	Dr'g'ts.
Baldwinsville	S. C. Suydam	Druggist.
Batavia	E. M. Jewell	Druggist.
Bath	F. N. DeCamp	Druggist.
Binghamton	S. L. Smith	Druggist.
Binghamton	The Elk Drug Co.	W. Drugs.
Buffalo	Becker & Wickser Co.	Har.
Buffalo	Blakesley & Koch Co.	Har.
Canton	Geo. S. Rogers	Druggist.
Canton	Don M. Spencer	Druggist.
Catskill	P. C. Lewis	Agent.
Corning	Cole & Mathews	Druggists.
Cortland	W. J. Perkins	Druggist.
Danville	G. Bastian	Druggist.
Dunkirk	Monroe's Pharmacy	
Fort Plain	F. G. Bartlett	Agent.
Geneva	W. H. Partridge	Druggist.
Glens Falls	Ames & Baldwin	Druggists.
Glens Falls	H. R. Leavens & Co.	C'r'ges.
Goshen	Power & Co.	Druggists.
Hoosick Falls	W. L. Thorpe	Druggist.
Hornellsville	C. H. Young	Druggist.
Hudson	A. McKinstrey & Son	Drgs.
Ilion	B. A. Russell & Co.	Dr'g'ts.
Ithaca	White & Burdick	Drug'sts.
Jamestown	Jamestown Pharmacy	
Johnstown	W. A. Livingston	Druggist.
Kingston	Cooper & Hardenburgh	Drg.
Lansingburg	H. W. Wood	Druggist.
Little Falls	G. R. Cardwell	Druggist.
Lockport	Fred. K. Sweet	Druggist.

Lyons	Moore & Moore	Druggists.
Middletown	J. E. Mills	Druggist.
Mt. Morris	H. W. Miller	Druggist.
Newburgh	Isaac C. Chapman.	Druggist.
Newburgh	Jas. H. Clancy	Horseman.
New Rochelle	J. J. & T. P. Kerwin	Drgts.
New York	The C. N. Crittenton Co.	Whol. Pat. Med.
New York	C. M. Moseman & Bro.	Har.
New York	J. Newton Van Ness Co.	Har.
Niagara Falls	Peter R. Croy	Druggist.
Norwich	Fred. Mitchell	Druggist.
Oak Hill	Fred. L. Pratt	Agent.
Ogdensburg	F. Howard Markham	Drgst.
Olean	Dr. Coon Drug Co.	
Oneonta	A. D. Rowe	Druggist.
Oswego	C. H. Butler	Druggist.
Penn Van	J. F. Bridgeman	Harness.
Plattsburg	Smith & La Rocque	Drgts.
Port Jervis	T. R. Anderson & Co.	Drgts.
Pottsdam	Brown & Perrin	Druggists.
Poughkeepsie	Barnes Bros.	Druggists.
Ritchfield Springs	Willard A. Smith	Druggists.
Rochester	E. H. Davis & Co.	W. Drugs.
Rochester	The Paine Drug Co.	W. Dr.
Rochester	J. K. Post & Co.	Wh. Drugs.
Rome	Broughton & Graves	Drgts.
Saratoga Springs	W. H. Walker	Druggist.
Syracuse	C. W. Snow & Co.	W. Drugs.
Syracuse	C. Hubbard, Son & Co.	W.D.
Ticonderoga	E. T. Wilcox & Co.	Dr'g'ts.
Troy	John L. Thompson, Sons & Co.	Whol. Drugs.
Troy	Polk & Calder Drug Co.	W.D.
Utica	Howarth & Ballard.	Drug'ts.
Waterloo	J. E. Batsford & Son.	Drgts.

Watertown ....J. K. Moffett........Harness.
Westchester ....M. R. Baxter & Son.Harness.

NORTH CAROLINA.

Graham ....L. B. Holt & Co..Gen. Store.
Raleigh ....W. C. McMackin........V. S.
Scotland Neck ....E. T. Whitehead & Co..Drg.

NORTH DAKOTA.

Fargo ....Sabin & Sabin.....Druggists.

OHIO.

Alliance ....Geo. R. Diver......Druggist.
Akron ....H. C. Blocker.......Druggist.
Bellefontaine ....G. M. Frazer.......Druggist.
Bryan ....Mrs. F. M. Carter..Druggist.
Bucyrus ....Farquhar Bros. ...Druggists.
Bowling Green ....J. C. Lincoln & Son...Drgts.
Canton ....Geo. C. Lindsay....Harness.
Chillicothe ....John A. Nipgen....Druggist.
Cincinnati ....J. D. Park, Son & Co..W.Dr.
Cincinnati ....Hale, Justis & Co...Wh. Dr.
Cincinnati ....G. S. Ellis & Son....Harness.
Circleville ....Evans & Krimmell..Dr'g'ts.
Cleveland ....Benton, Myers & Co.Wh. Dr.
Cleveland ....Strong, Cobb & Co..Wh. Dr.
Cleveland ....W. A. King.........Harness.
Columbus ....Kauffman-Lattimer Co.W.D.
Columbus ....M. D. Coons & Co.Druggists.
Coshocton ....C. E. Anderson.....Druggist.
Dayton ....D. Leonhard & Son..Harn's.
Dayton ....J. Harry Good..Blacksmith.
Defiance ....N. G. Woodward...Druggist.
Delaware ....W. T. Joyner.......Druggist.

Delphos	Boehmer & Floding.	Drug'ts.
Eaton	W. P. Brookins & Son.	Drg.
Elyria	Henry J. Eady	Druggist.
Findlay	Oak Pharmacy	
Fremont	C. R. McCulloch	Druggist.
Gallipolis	G. A. Rodel	Druggist.
Greenville	D. O. Klinger	Druggist.
Jefferson	C. H. Case	Druggist.
Kenton	J. A. Rogers	Druggist.
Lebanon	J. P. Rawles	Druggist.
Lima	J. D. Jones	Harness.
Lindenville	F. C. B. Wilcox	V. S.
Mansfield	F. W. Durno	Harness.
Marietta	J. W. Dysle & Co.	Druggists.
Marietta	H. F. Curtis	Druggist.
Marysville	W. H. Armstrong	Druggist.
Massillon	E. S. Craig	Druggist.
Middletown	McCoy & Kitchen	Drug'sts
Minerva	W. D. Roller	Druggist.
Mt. Vernon	Scribner & Co	Druggists.
Newark	Frank D. Hall	Druggist.
New London	S. W. Flemming	Druggist.
New Philadelphia	Brister & Le Page	Drug'ts.
North Benton	A. E. Strong	Gen. Store.
Norwalk	R. S. Wooster	Druggist.
Painesville	Moodey's Pharmacy	
Piqua	Prof. J. W. Allen	Trainer.
Potsdam	L. Ammon & Sons.	G. Store.
Rock Creek	G. H. Ray	Trainer.
Salem	M. S. Hawkins	Druggist.
Salem	Trimble Bros.	Druggists.
Sandusky	Melville Bros.	Druggists.
Sandusky	Frank Wagner	Harness.
Sidney	H. W. Thompson	Druggist.
Springfield	Theo. Troupe	Druggist.

Steubenville ....Beall & Steele.....Druggists.
Tiffin ....E. B. Hubbard.....Druggist.
Toledo ....The Walding, Kinnan &
                         Marvin Co....Whol. Drugs.
Urbana ....Converse & Hunter.Drug'ts.
Van Wert ....F. P. Hill & Co...Druggists.
Warren ....McClure & Voit...Druggists.
Washington C. H......C. B. Henderson...Druggist.
Wellsville ....Wm. M. Bright....Druggist.
Wooster ....W. A. Wilson......Druggist.
Xenia ....Geo. Galloway .....Druggist.
Youngstown ....The Folsom-Thayer Co..Drg.
Zanesville ....H. M. Widney......Druggist.

OREGON.

Portland ....Woodard, Clarke & Co.W. D.
Portland ....Blumaner-Frank Drug Co.
                         ....Whol. Drugs.

PENNSYLVANIA.

Allentown ....Peters & Smith....Druggists.
Apollo ....T. A. Cochran......Druggist.
Bethlehem ....Paul Kempsmith ..Druggist.
Bradford ....Thompson & Wood.W.&R.D.
Bristol ....L. A. Hoguet........Druggist.
Butler ....J. F. Balph..........Druggist.
Butler ....John Kemper ....Harness.
Carbondale ....B. A. Kelly.........Druggist.
Carlisle ....W. F. Horn.........Druggist.
Chambersburg ....Wm. G. Greenawalt.Drug'st.
Chester ....J. C. Kepner........Druggist.
Clearfield ....E. W. Graham.....Druggist.
Coatsville ....Franklin Megargee.....V. S.
Columbia ....W. L. Bear.........Harness.
Columbia .... H. W. Zeamer......Druggist.

American Veterinary Remedy. 73

Corry	H. W. Gretzler	Livery.
Danville	Leniger Bros.	Druggists.
Du Bois	Vosburg Drug Co.	
East Canton	E. G. Van Dyke	V. S.
Erie	Haviland & Hunter	Drug'ts.
Franklin	Martin & Epley	Druggists.
Germantown, Phila.	John J. Campbell	Harness.
Harrisburg	Geo. A. Gorgas	Druggist.
Hazleton	Diamond Drug Store	
Hazleton	H. L. Smith	Druggist.
Huntingdon	H. E. Steele	Druggist.
Johnstown	Sam'l Lenhart, Jr.	Harness.
Kittanning	Geo. S. Rohrer	Druggist.
Lancaster	Chas. A. Heinitsh	Druggist.
Lancaster	Philip Rudy	Harness.
Lebanon	Dr. G. Ross & Co.	Druggists.
Lebanon	Lemberger & Co.	Druggists.
Milton	Brown's Drug Store	
Norristown	Wm. Stahler	Druggist.
Philadelphia	Smith, Kline, French & Co.	Whol. Drugs.
Philadelphia	Geo. DeB. Keim & Co.	Har.
Philipsburg	S. S. Crissman	Druggist.
Pittsburg	W. J. Gilmore & Co.	Wh. Dr.
Pittsburg	Geo. A. Kelly & Co.	Wh. Dr.
Pittsburg	Jos. Loughrey & Son	Har.
Pottsville	J. H. Rabenau	Druggist.
Reading	J. B. Raser	W. & R. Drugs.
Reading	McCurdy & Durham	Drgts.
Scranton	A. W. Musgrave	Druggists.
Shamokin	T. R. Clarkson & Co.	Dr'g'ts.
Shamokin	J. H. Conley & Co.	Drug'ts.
Sunbury	Dr. P. H. Renn	Druggist.
Tarentum	James M. Esler	Druggist.
Tillotson	C. A. Davis	Agent.
Tionesta	S. S. Canfield	Agent.

Tyrone ....Frank M. Musser..Druggist.
Washington ....L. S. Vowell........Druggist.
Williamsport ....Duble & Cornell..Druggists.
York ....Wm. Smith & Co....Wh. Dr.

RHODE ISLAND.

Providence ....Blanding & Blanding..W. D.
Providence ....The T. W. Rounds Co..Har.

SOUTH CAROLINA.

Jacksonboro ..........W.B.Bischoff & Bro.Gen. St.
Seneca ....Stribling Drug Co............

TENNESSEE.

Clarksville ....Owen & Moore....Druggists.
Columbus ....A. B. Rains........Druggist.
Chattanooga ....Chattanooga Drug Co........
Memphis ....Van Vleet-Mansfield Drug
                         Co. ....Whol. Drugs.
Memphis ....Lilly Carriage Co...Harness.
Murfreesboro ....H. H. Kerr..........Druggist.
Nashville ....De Moville & Co..Druggists.

TEXAS.

Austin ....Kluge Bros. ....Harness.
Dallas ....J. W. Crowdus Drug Co.
Dallas ....Trice Saddlery Co............
El Paso ....J. Caldwell, Propr. Star Sta.
Fort Worth ....H. W. Williams & Co..W.Dr.
Houston ....R. F. George..........Agent.
San Antonio *.........C. Schasse ....Druggist.

VERMONT.

Barre ....John Trow ....Carriages.
Burlington ....F. H. Parker & Co..Drug'ts.

Burlington ....W. H. Zottman & Co..Drgts.
Lowell ....Will L. Kinsley........Agent.
Rutland ....Miner & Thomas..Druggists.

VIRGINIA.

Danville ....F. Clarke ....Druggist.
Lynchburg ....M. E. Doyle........Harness.
Norfolk ....Burrows, Martin & Co.Drgts
Richmond ....Owens & Miner Drug Co.
 ....Whol. Drugs.
Sharps Wharf ....Frederick Downing.Ag. Imp.

WEST VIRGINIA.

Wheeling ....Chas. R. Goetze....Druggist.

WISCONSIN.

Ashland ....G. W. Harrison....Druggist.
Chippewa Falls........Good Luck Drug Co..........
Eau Claire ....Schwahn & Co......Harness.
Fon-du-Lac ....O. H. Musgat........Harness.
Green Bay ....Cauwenburgh Bros....Drgts.
Janesville ....E. B. Heimstreet...Druggist.
Janesville ....J. B. Smith............Agent.
La Crosse ....T. H. Spence Drug Co........
Madison ....A. H. Hollister.....Druggist.
Manitowoc ....Henry Henrichs ...Druggist.
Milwaukee ....Jerman, Pflueger & Keuhm-
 sted Co.......Whol. Drugs.
Milwaukee .... Drake Bros. & Co..Wh. Dr
Neenah ....M. E. Barnett & Co...Drgts.
Oshkosh ....Guenther's Pharmacy ....
Oshkosh ....J. T. Chase..........Harness.
Racine ....F. Harbridge ......Druggist.
Sheboygan ....M. R. Zaegel & Co....Drgts.

Spencer ....E. Heath ....Druggist.
Waukesha ....:.....A. E. Estburg......Druggist.
West Superior ....H. O. Thompson....Harness.

ONTARIO.

Hamilton ....Parke & Parke...Druggists.
Toronto ....The Lyman Bros. Co.Wh.Dr.

QUEBEC.

Montreal ....Lyman, Sons & Co..Wh. Dr.

NEW BRUNSWICK.

St. Johns .... T. B. Barker & Son..Wh.Dr.

Price—Large bottles, $2.00; small bottles, $1.00.

Sole manufacturers—H. S. Bossart & Co., Latrobe, Pa., U. S. A.

When you ask your dealer for Dr. Turnbull's CURINE, if he does not have it in stock, insist on him getting it from his jobber or the manufacturers. Don't allow him to talk you into buying any other remedy, and if he does not get it for you, order it yourself from the manufacturers.

RATES OF POSTAGE.

Postal cards, 1 cent each, go without further charge to all parts of the United States and Canada. Cards for foreign countries (within the postal union), 2 cents each. Postal cards are unmailable with any writing or printing on the address side, except the direction, or with anything pasted upon or attached to them.

All letters, to all parts of the United States, Canada and Mexico, 2 cents for each ounce or fraction thereof.

Local, or "drop letters," that is, for the city or town where deposited, 2 cents where the carrier system is adopted, and 1 cent where there is no carrier system.

First Class.—Letters and all other written matter, whether sealed or unsealed, and all other matter, sealed, nailed, sewed or fastened in any manner so that it cannot be easily examined, 2 cents for each ounce or fraction thereof.

Second Class.—Only for publishers and news agents, 1 cent per pound. Newspapers and periodicals (regular publications) can be mailed by the public at the rate of 1 cent for each 4 ounces or fraction thereof.

Third Class.—Printed matter, in unsealed wrappers only (all matter enclosed in notched envelopes must pay letter rates), 1 cent for each 2 ounces or fraction thereof, which must be fully prepaid. This includes books, circulars, chromos, engravings, handbills, lithographs, music, pamphlets, proofsheets and manuscript accompanying the same, reproductions by the electric pen, hektograph, metallograph, papyrograph, and, in short, any reproduction upon paper, by any process except handwriting, the copying press, typewriter and the neostyle process. Limit of weight, 4 pounds, except for a single book, which may weigh more.

Fourth Class.—All mailable matter not included in the three preceding classes, which is so prepared for mailing as to be easily withdrawn from the wrapper and examined, 1 cent per ounce or fraction thereof. Limit of weight, 4 pounds. Full payment compulsory.

FOREIGN POSTAGE.

The rates for letters are for the half-ounce or fraction thereof 5 cents each, and those for newspapers for 2 ounces or fraction thereof, 1 cent.

WORLD'S RECORDS.

The following table of champion records is compiled from the published volumes of the Year Book, with the results of 1897 added. The table contains much valuable information, and in a condensed and ready reference form:

TROTTING.

One mile—Alix, b m, by Patronage (1894)......2:03¾
Two miles—Greenlander, blk h, by Princeps (1893) 4:32
Three miles—Nightengale, ch m, by Mambrino King (1893) 6:55½
Fastest mare—Alix, b, by Patronage (1894)....2:03¾
Fastest stallion—Directum, blk, by Director (1893) 2:05¼
Fastest gelding—Azote, b, by Whips (1895)......2:04¾
Fastest yearling filly—Pansy McGregor, b, by Fergus McGregor (1893).....................2:23¾
Fastest yearling colt—Adbell, b, by Advertiser (1894) 2:23
Fastest two-year colt—Arion, b, by Electioneer (1891) ....,2:10¾
Fastest two-year-old filly—Janie T., b, by Bow Bells (1897) 2:14
Fastest two-year-old gelding—Fred S. Moody, ch, by Guy Wilkes (1895)......................2:18
Fastest three-year-old filly—Fantasy, b, by Chimes (1893) 2:08¾
Fastest three-year-old colt—Arion, b, by Electioneer (1892) 2:10½
Fastest three-year-old gelding—Preston, gr, by Ponce de Leon (1897)........................2:13¼
Fastest four-year-old colt—Directum, blk c, by Director (1893).............................2:05¼
Fastest four-year-old filly—Fantasy, b, by Chimes (1894) 2:06
Fastest four-year-old gelding—The Monk, b, by Chimes (1897)..............................2:08¼

Fastest five-year-old stallion—Ralph Wilkes, ch, by Red Wilkes (1894................2:06¾
Fastest five-year-old mare—Fantasy, b, by Chimes (1895) 2:07
Fastest five-year-old gelding—Mosul, b, by Sultan (1897) 2:09¼

TROTTING—IN RACES.

Fastest heat—Alix, b m, by Patronage (1894); Directum, blk h, by Director (1893)..........2:05¼
Fastest heat, gelding—Azote, b, by Whips (1895)2:05½
Fastest heat, yearling—Pansy McGregor, b f, by Fergus McGregor (1893)................2:23¾
Fastest heat, two-year-old—Jupe, b c, by Allie Wilkes (1896) 2:13¾
Fastest heat, three-year-old—Fantasy, b f, by Chimes (1892) 2:08¾
Fastest heat, four-year-old—Directum, blk c, by Director (1893)................2:05¼
Fastest heat, five-year-old—Wm. Penn, br h, by Santa Claus (1895)................2:07¼

TROTTING—TO WAGON.

One mile—David B., ch g, by Young Jim (1896).2:12½
One mile (in a race)—Alfred S., b g, by Elmo (1890) 2:16¾
Two miles—Dexter, br g, by Hambletonian (1865) 4:56¼

TROTTING—UNDER SADDLE.

One mile—Great Eastern, b g, by Walkill Chief (1877) 2:15¾
Two miles—Geo. M. Patchen, b h, by Cassius M. Clay (1863) 4:56

TROTTING—WITH RUNNING MATE.

One mile (against time)—Ayers P., ch g, by Prosper Merimee (1893)................2:03½
One mile (in race)—Frank, b g, by Abraham (1883) 2:08½

TROTTING—TEAMS.

One mile—Belle Hamlin, br m, by Almont, Jr., (Hamlin's), and Honest George, b g, by Albert (1892) 2:12¼
One mile (in a race)—Roseleaf, blk f, 4, by Gold Leaf, and Sally Simmons, b f, 4, by Simmons (1894) 2:15¼

TEAMS—THREE ABREAST.

One mile—Belle Hamlin, br m; Globe, b g, and Justina, b m, by Almont, Jr., (1891)..........2:14

TEAMS—FOUR-IN-HAND.

One mile—Damiana, ch m; Bellnut, ch g; Maud V., ch m, and Nutspra, ch m, all by Nutmeg (1896) 2:30

TROTTING—HALF-MILE TRACK.

One mile—Dandy Jim, gr g, by Young Jim (1897) 2:10¼
One mile, by a mare—Bush, blk, by Alcyone (1897) 2:11¼
One mile, by a stallion—Pat L., b c, 4, by Republican (1896) 2:10
One mile, in a race—Dandy Jim, gr g, by Young Jim (1897) 2:10¼
One mile, by team—Lynn Bourbon, br m, by Bourbon Wilkes, and Bertie Girl, b m, by Jay Bird (1897) 2:16¾

PACING.

One mile—Star Pointer, b h, by Brown Hal (1897) 1:59¼
Two miles—Chehalis, blk h, by Altamont (1897) (first mile 2:09, second mile 2:10¼)............4:19¼
Fastest stallion—Star Pointer, b, by Brown Hal (1897) 1:59¼
Fastest gelding—Robert J., b, by Hartford (1894) 2:01½
Fastest mare—Bessie Bonehill, gr, by Empire Wilkes (1897); Lottie Loraine, b, by Gambetta Wilkes (1897)...2:05¾

Fastest yearling, filly—Belle Acton, b, by
  Shadeland Onward (1892).......................2:20¾
Fastest yearling, colt—Rosedale, b, by Sidney
  (1893) 2:22
Fastest yearling, gelding—Rollo, gr, by Jerome
  Eddy (1891) 2:28½
Fastest two-year-old, colt—Directly, blk, by
  Direct (1894) 2:07¾
Fastest two-year-old, filly—Lena Hill, blk, by
  Wm. M. Hill (1893).............................2:12¾
Fastest three-year-old, colt—Directly, blk, by
  Direct (1895) 2:07¼
Fastest three-year-old, filly—Miss Rita, ch, by
  J. J. Audubon (1895)...........................2:09¾
Fastest three-year-old, gelding—Agitato, b, by
  Steinway (1896); King of Diamonds, b, by
  Velocity (1896) 2:09¼
Fastest four-year-old, colt—Online, b, by
  Shadeland Onward (1894)........................2:04
Fastest four-year-old, filly—Aileen, b, by Ga-
  zette (1895) 2:07½
Fastest four-year-old, gelding—W. Wood, b, by
  Steinway (1892) 2:07
Fastest five-year-old, stallion—John R. Gen-
  try, b, by Ashland Wilkes (1894)...............2:03¾
Fastest five-year-old, gelding—Robert J., b, by
  Hartford (1893); Frank Agan, b, by Mika-
  gan (1895) 2:05¾
Fastest five-year-old, mare—Bessie Bonehill,
  gr, by Empire Wilkes (1897)....................2:05¾

PACING—IN RACES.

Fastest heat, stallion—Star Pointer, b, by
  Brown Hal (1897)...............................2:00½
Fastest heat, gelding—Robert J., b, by Hart-
  ford (1894) 2:02½
Fastest heat, mare—Bessie Bonehill, gr, by
  Empire Wilkes (1897); Lottie Loraine, b, by
  Gambetta Wilkes (1897).........................2:05¾
Fastest heat, yearling—Belle Acton, b f, by
  Shadeland Onward (1892)........................2:20¼
Fastest heat, two-year-old—Symboleer, b c, by
  Campbell's Electioneer (1894) 2:11

Fastest heat, three-year-old—Judge Hurt, b c, by Wm. M. Hill (1895); Agitato, b g, by Steinway (1896); Sulphide, b c, by Superior (1896); King of Diamonds, b g, by Velocity (1896); Searchlight, br c, by Darknight (1897).2:09¼
Fastest heat, four-year-old—Be Sure, b c, by Bessemer (1895); Ananias, b c, by Patron (1897) 2:06¾
Fastest heat, five-year-old—John R. Gentry, b h, by Ashland Wilkes (1894).................. 2:03¾

PACING—TO WAGON.

One mile—Joe Patchen, blk h, by Patchen Wilkes (1897) 2:04¾
One mile (in a race)—Joe Patchen, blk h, by Patchen Wilkes (1896)........................ 2:11¼

PACING—UNDER SADDLE.

One mile—Johnston, b g, by Joe Bassett (1888).2:13
One mile (in a race)—Billy Boyce, b g, by Corbeau (1868) 2:14¼
Two miles—Bowery Boy, br g, pedigree untraced (1839) 5:04½

PACING—WITH RUNNING MATE.

One mile—Flying Jib, b g, by Algona (1894)....1:58¼

PACING—TEAMS.

One mile—John R. Gentry, b h, by Ashland Wilkes and Robert J., b g, by Hartford (1897) 2:08
One mile (in a race)—Belle Button, br m, and Tom Ryder, br g, by Alexander Button (1892) 2:16½

PACING—HALF-MILE TRACK.

One mile—Joe Patchen, blk h, by Patchen Wilkes (1896) 2:04¼
One mile, by a gelding—Robert J., b, by Hartford (1897) 2:05¾
One mile, by a mare—Pearl C., b, by Roy Wilkes (1897) 2:08
One mile (in a race)—Pearl C., b, by Roy Wilkes (1897) 2:08

FREE!
TO HORSEMEN.

Our beautiful catalogue containing nearly 800 illustrations of useful Turf Goods and Harness of every description, at lower prices than they have heretofore been offered, will be mailed absolutely **FREE** to any address on application. Write for one at once and mention this book. ♣ ♣ ♣ ♣ ♣

We Will Save You Many a Dollar During the Season.

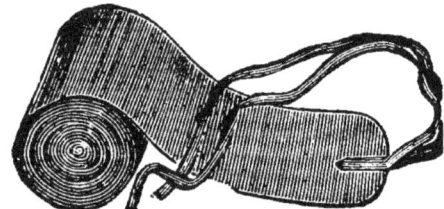

BEST QUALITY,
9 Ft. (Belmont)

DERBY BANDAGES

44c. For Complete Set of Four, same as others ask 75c. and $1.00 for.

G. S. ELLIS & SON,

Largest and Lowest Priced Manufacturers of

HARNESS and TURF GOODS
IN THE WORLD.

430 Main St., = CINCINNATI, O.

A Valuable Book For Horsemen Free.

TUTTLE & CLARK will send free of charge their magnificent Catalogue illustrating and describing all kinds of harness and horse goods, in beautiful colors, and include with same pictures of some valuable horses and other pictures suitable for decorating stables. They will also send their wholesale discount book to those who mention where they saw this advertisement. Send 15c. to part pay the express charges. The book weighs 2 lbs., has 226 pages, and is the finest ever published. Address, TUTTLE & CLARK, 216 Jefferson Avenue, Detroit, Mich.

S. TOOMEY & CO.'S
POPULAR SULKIES.

BUILT LIKE A WATCH.

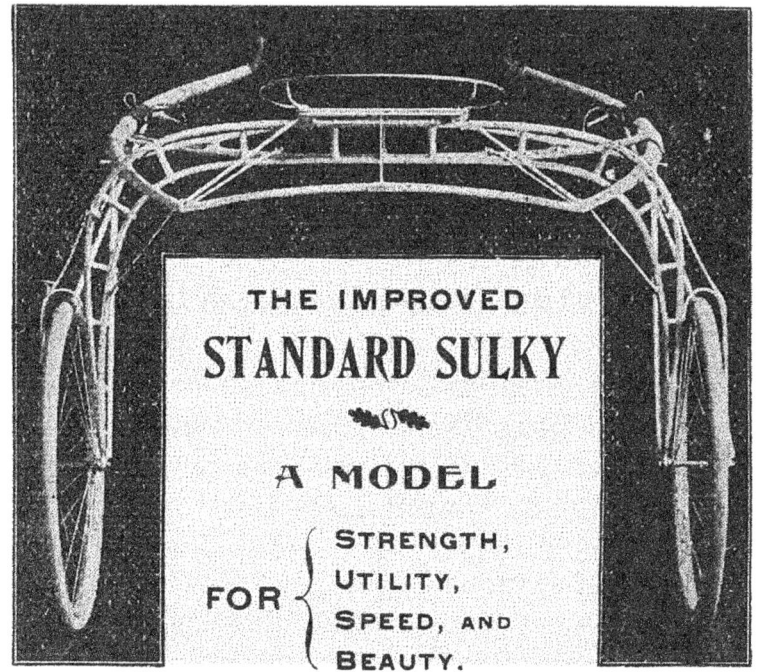

THE IMPROVED
STANDARD SULKY

A MODEL

FOR { STRENGTH, UTILITY, SPEED, AND BEAUTY.

The Greatest Record Breaker.
The Greatest Money Maker.

THE TOOMEY CARTS
FINEST ON TWO WHEELS
Neat, Light and Strong.

Positively the easiest riding cart in the world.
Send for illustrations of other style sulkies and carts.

S. TOOMEY & CO.,
Canal Dover, O., U. S. A.

CURINE ALLERTON,
30676.

Black horse, foaled 1895; will be 16¼ hands.

SIRED BY THE GREAT

ALLERTON, 2:09¼,

THE WORLD'S CHAMPION SIRE OF HIS AGE.

Dam ESTELLE DAYTON............by ARSACES, 6506
(Sire of 3 in 2:20 list.)

2nd dam ROSE HILL............by YOUNG JIM, 2009
(Sire of 40 in list.)

3d dam DORA PATCHEN...by TOM PATCHEN, 3996
Son of GEO. M. Patchen, 30.

Here is a grand individual, and he is four times inbred to the great George Wilkes through his best sons. At the time of the publication of this book (June, 1898) he could show a 2:20 clip over a half-mile track.

SERVICE FEE, $25 TO INSURE.

For particulars, address,

H. S. BOSSART & CO.,
LATROBE, PA.

EVERYTHING FOR

.. YOUR HORSE—

☘ QUICK. ☘

What you cannot find elsewhere

you can find at **MOSEMAN'S**

WRITE AND SEE.

C. M. MOSEMAN & BRO.

Horse Furnishing Goods from
all parts of the world.

SALESROOM:

126 and 128 CHAMBERS ST.,

NEW YORK.

BRANCHES

LONDON.   PARIS.   BERLIN.   MOSCOW.

DISINFECTING:

Stables, like every other place, should be kept clean, and all vermin and offensive odors destroyed. To do this cheaply, safely and effectively, use the Modern Disinfectant,

CREOLOL

A PURE COAL TAR PRODUCT,

An Antiseptic, Germicide, Deodorizing Disinfectant. Invaluable in treating Sores, Burns, and Bruises. In use in hundreds of stables. Write for Booklet.

AMERICAN CREOLOL CO.
LATROBE, PA., U.S.A.

IN USE IN ALL PRINCIPAL HOSPITALS.

THE T. W. ROUNDS CO.,

101 to 109 North Main Street,

PROVIDENCE, R. I.

MANUFACTURERS

..AND..

IMPORTERS

HARNESS, SADDLERY,

Horse Furnishings

..AND..

Turf Goods.

..MAKERS OF THE..

"Rounds" Track Harness

$25.00.

STATE AGENTS FOR GILLIAM HORSE BOOTS,

J. O'KANE'S "CALIFORNIA" HORSE BOOTS,

—AND—

CURINE.

Everything for the Horse and Stable.

SPECIAL INDUCEMENTS TO HORSEMEN.

Catalogue of Horse Boots and Turf Goods mailed free.

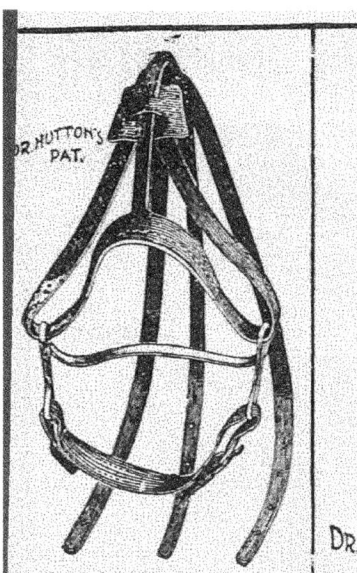 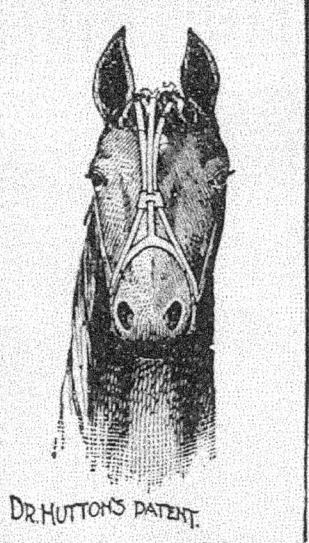

Dr. HUTTON'S CHECKING DEVICE is the only check for Pullers or Bit-Fighters that the bearing can be regulated on either Chin Strap or Bit. Used by Ed. F. Geers and other first-class trainers.

CHECK COMPLETE. $5.50.

J. J. FOSTER,

MANUFACTURER OF

HARNESS AND SADDLERY

.. AND ..

JOBBER OF TURF GOODS SPECIALTIES.

Special Wholesale and Retail Selling Agents for

Dr. HUTTON'S CHECKING DEVICE

Gilliams', J. O'Kane's, and J. Fennell's

HORSE BOOTS.

Campbell's and Harrold's Hoof Oils,

CURINE, PURE WITCH HAZEL, LAMB'S EYE SHIELDS.

CHICAGO CLIPPERS, 98 M., $10.75; 97 M., $15.
ASHTON SALT SACKS, COOLERS,
Blankets, Hobbles, Toe Weights,
and everything for the horse at the lowest possible price.

511 MAIN ST., KANSAS CITY, MO.

LITTLEFIELD'S ENAMEL DRESSING

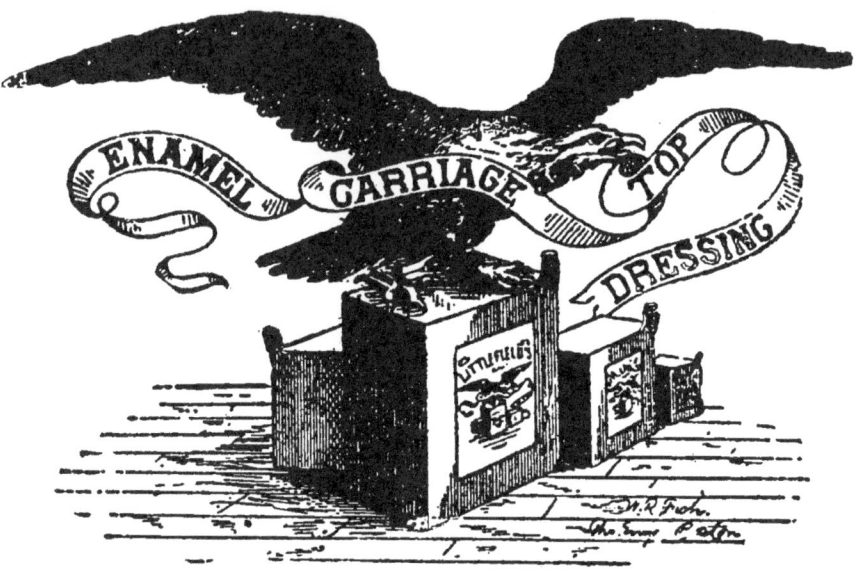

FOR CARRIAGE TOPS AND DASHES.

The most perfect Leather Dressing in the world.
It contains more **Oil** than any Enamel Dressing sold
It **Penetrates, Softens** and **Preserves** the leather.
It leaves a **Fine Enamel Finish.**
It is equally as good for Enamel or Rubber Cloth.
It dries out of the way of dust over night.
It is very **durable,** and makes an old top as good as new.
It is the **cheapest,** as it covers one-fourth more surface than any Dressing on the market.

PRICE LIST.

From ½ Gallon to 5 Gallon Cans...per Gal. $ 4.00
Quarts..per Doz. 15.00
Pints .... "   9.00
Half Pints .... "   6.00

☞ No charge for cans.   Discount to the Trade.

WALDO LITTLEFIELD,
MANUFACTURER,
WEST ACTON, MASS.

HORSE CLIPPING MACHINES

LIGHT WEIGHT Hand Power. **$15**

HEAVY WEIGHT, Hand Power **$20**

THE	THE	THE
BEST.	**REST.**	**TEST.**

There are two kinds of Horse Clipping Machines: The Best—and the Rest. The trouble is they all look alike. And when the rest dress like the best, who's to tell them apart? Well, "the tree is known by it's fruit." That's an old test and a safe one. And the taller the tree the deeper the root. That's another test. What's the root,—the record of these machines. The one with the deepest root is the "GILLETTE." The one with the richest fruit—that, too, is the "GILLETTE." If you want to get the best Machine of your dealer, here's an infallible rule: Ask for the best and you will get a "GILLETTE." Ask for a "GILLETTE" and you will get the best.

STILL HAVE DOUBTS?   SEND FOR OUR CATALOGUE.

IT KILLS DOUBTS AND CURES DOUBTERS.

GILLETTE CLIPPING MACHINE CO.

110, 112 & 114 West 32nd St., NEW YORK.

No. 2 Shows Tongs for Applying Expander.

No. 4 Shows Saw for Opening Heel.

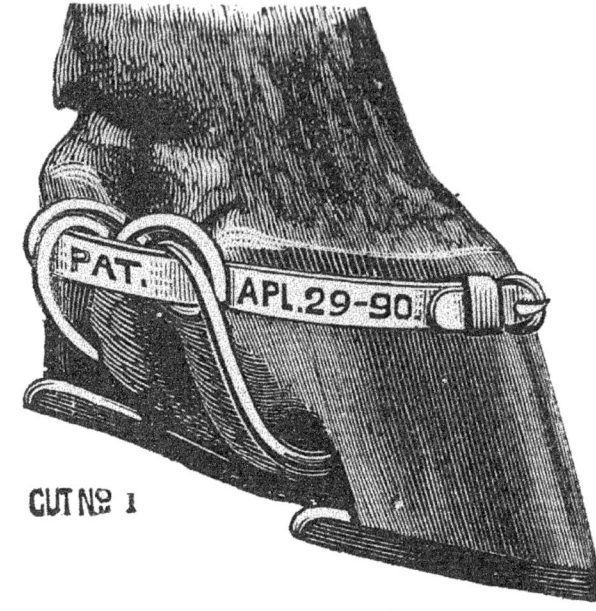

Shows Foot with Expander in.

FORT MEADE, S. Dakota.
HEADQUARTERS 8th U. S. CAVALRY:
    Mackey's Hoof Expanders were applied to nine horses of the regiment, suffering from Chronic Lameness, Contracted Hoofs, Corns, Side-bones, Hoof-cracks, etc. Eight of these horses were free from lameness in ten days afterwards.   M. J. TREACY,
                            Veterinarian 8th U. S. Cavalry.
Graduate Royal College Veterinary Surgeons, England.

                      SCIO, N. Y., April 23, 1898.
S. W. MACKEY, ESQ. Baltimore, Md.:
    DEAR SIR—Goods received all O. K. I cured one case of contracted feet with navicular lameness, which had been lame for one and a half years. I made the cure in six days. It was for Doctor T. F. Major, M. D., Scio, N. Y. The feet opened one-half inch when the Expanders were applied, and another half inch when they were in six days. This horse was on pasture all last Summer and was no better in the Fall. He was so lame that he had not tried to use him for over a year. Now he is the best horse he has and he uses him every day. The Doctor says they have worked wonders. You can give anyone his or my address for references. I enclose P. O. Order for one dozen pairs of Springs. Send by Express. They are all right, as all I have used are relieving lameness in every case. I am, My Dear Sir,
      Most respectfully,   C. A. SIMMONS, D. V. S.

Write for Circulars and Letters, so as to know how to order, to

S. W. MACKEY, Foot Specialist,
1126 E. Baltimore St.   **BALTIMORE, MD.**

INDEX.

	PAGE NO.
Abscesses	37
Big Leg—Lymphangitis	32
Blood Spavin	7
Bone Spavin	6
Bots	27
Broken Wind	14
Calk Wounds	30
Canker	43
Capped Elbow	16
Capped Hock	19
Chafing	34
Cocked Ankles	15
Contracted Heels	44
Corns	20
Cracked Heels	31
Cramp Colic	4
Cramp of the Leg	38
Curb	24
Dentition	3
Diarrhea	39
Distemper	47
Epizoody	21
Farcy	41
Fistulæ	9
Flatulent Colic	4
Founder	8
Frog Bruise	46
Glanders	41
Heaves	14
Hip Joint Lameness	39
Indigestion	33
Influenza	21
Irregularities of Teeth	3
Knuckling	15
Laminitas	8
Lampas	3
Lock-Jaw	23
Lung Fever	17
Mange	48
Masturbation	49
Navicular Disease	13
Overreach	28

THIS BOOK IS DUE ON THE LAST DATE STAMPED BELOW

AN INITIAL FINE OF 25 CENTS
WILL BE ASSESSED FOR FAILURE TO RETURN THIS BOOK ON THE DATE DUE. THE PENALTY WILL INCREASE TO 50 CENTS ON THE FOURTH DAY AND TO $1.00 ON THE SEVENTH DAY OVERDUE.

(BIOLOGY LIBRARY)

Bossart, H. S. & co.
 The principal diseases
of the horse

268440   SF951
         B6

JUN 15 1935   JUN 8 935
NOV 30 1941   DEC 1 194

SF951
B6
BIOLOGY
LIBRARY

268440

UNIVERSITY OF CALIFORNIA LIBRARY